The Legalization of Drugs

In the United States today, the use or possession of many drugs is a criminal offense. Can these criminal laws be justified? What are the best reasons to punish or not to punish drug users? These are the fundamental issues debated in this book by two prominent philosophers of law. Douglas Husak argues in favor of drug decriminalization by clarifying the meaning of crucial terms such as *legalize, decriminalize,* and *drugs*; and by identifying the standards by which alternative drug policies should be assessed. He critically examines the reasons typically offered in favor of the current approach and explains why decriminalization is preferable. Peter de Marneffe argues against drug legalization, demonstrating why drug prohibition, especially the prohibition of heroin, is necessary to protect young people from self-destructive drug use. If the empirical assumptions of this argument are sound, he reasons, drug prohibition is perfectly compatible with our rights to liberty.

Douglas Husak is Professor of Philosophy at Rutgers University and Professor of Law at Rutgers Law School. He is the author of many articles and books, including *Philosophy of Criminal Law, Drugs and Rights,* and *Legalize This! The Case for Decriminalizing Drugs*.

Peter de Marneffe is Associate Professor of Philosophy at Arizona State University. A recipient of postdoctoral fellowships at the University Center for Human Values at Princeton University and at the Program in Ethics and the Professions at Harvard University, he has published articles on liberty and liberalism in *Philosophy & Public Affairs* and *Ethics,* among other journals.

For and Against

General Editor: R. G. Frey

For and Against offers a new and exciting approach to the investigation of complex philosophical ideas and their impact on the way we think about a host of contemporary moral, social, and political issues. Two philosophical essays explore a topic of intense public interest from opposing points of view. This approach provides the reader with a balanced perspective on the topic; it also introduces the deep philosophical conflicts that underpin the differing views. The result is both a series of important statements on some of the most challenging questions facing our society and an introduction to moral, social, and political philosophy. Each essay is compact and nontechnical, yet avoids a simplistic, journalistic presentation of the topic.

Other books in the series:

David Schmidtz and Robert E. Goodin, *Social Welfare and Individual Responsibility*

Gerald Dworkin, R. G. Frey, and Sissela Bok, *Euthanasia and Physician-Assisted Suicide*

Christopher Heath Wellman and A. John Simmons, *Is There a Duty to Obey the Law?*

The Legalization of Drugs

Douglas Husak
Rutgers University

and

Peter de Marneffe
Arizona State University

CAMBRIDGE
UNIVERSITY PRESS

CAMBRIDGE UNIVERSITY PRESS
Cambridge, New York, Melbourne, Madrid, Cape Town, Singapore, São Paulo

Cambridge University Press
40 West 20th Street, New York, NY 10011-4211, USA

www.cambridge.org
Information on this title: www.cambridge.org/9780521837866

First published 2005

Printed in the United States of America

A catalog record for this publication is available from the British Library.

Library of Congress Cataloging in Publication Data

Husak, Douglas N., 1948–
The legalization of drugs / Douglas Husak, Peter de Marneffe.
   p.   cm. – (For and against)
Includes bibliographical references and index.
ISBN 0-521-83786-3 (hardcover) – ISBN 0-521-54686-9 (pbk.)
1. Drug legalization – United States.   2. Drugs of abuse – Law and legislation –
United States – Criminal provisions.   I. De Marneffe, Peter, 1957–   II. Title.
III. Series: For and against (Cambridge, England)
KF3890.H87   2005
364.1′77′0973 – dc22   2004027502

ISBN-13   978-0-521-83786-6 hardback
ISBN-10   0-521-83786-3 hardback

ISBN-13   978-0-521-54686-7 paperback
ISBN-10   0-521-54686-9 paperback

Contents

General Editor's Preface

SINCE the mid-1960s, the application of ethical theory to moral, social, political, and legal issues has formed a growing part of public life and of the philosophical curriculum. Except perhaps during the 1950s and the flowering of ordinary language philosophy, moral philosophers have always to some extent been concerned with the practical application of their theories. On the whole, however, they did little more than sketch implications or draw provisional conclusions with regard to practical issues based upon some distant familiarity with a few empirical facts. Today, the opposite is the case: They have come to immerse themselves in the subject matter of the issues with which they are normatively concerned, whether these come from law, medicine, business, or the affairs of social and political life. As a result, they have come to apply their theories with a much broader and deeper understanding of the factual setting within which the issues in question arise and have become of public concern.

Courses in applied ethics now figure throughout the philosophical curriculum, including, increasingly, within philosophy components of professional education. More and more periodicals – philosophical, professional, popular – devote space to medical and business ethics, to environmental and animal rights issues, to discussions of suicide, euthanasia, and physician-assisted suicide, to surrogate motherhood and the rights of children, to the ethics of war and the moral case for and against assisting famine victims, and so on. Indeed, new periodicals are devoted entirely to applied issues, from numerous environmental quarterlies to the vast number of journals in medical ethics that today feature a compendium of philosophical, medical, and sometimes popular authors writing on a diverse array of issues ultimately concerned with life, quality of life, and death.

What is striking about the *best* philosophical writing in all these areas (I concede that there is much chaff amongst the wheat) is that it is factually informed and methodologically situated in the subject areas under discussion, to a degree that enables specialists in those areas – be they doctors, lawyers, environmentalists, or the like – to see the material as both engaging and relevant. Yet, the writing is pitched at the level of the educated person, comparatively free of technicalities and jargon, and devoted to matters of public concern. Much of it, whether by philosophers or others, such as economists and political and social scientists, is known outside the academy and has had the effect, as it were, of taking philosophy into the public arena.

Interest in applied ethics will continue to grow as a result of technological/scientific developments, enacted social policies, and political/economic decisions. For example, genetic engineering raises a number of important moral issues, from those that concern human cloning, illnesses, and treatments to those that center around alteration in animal species and the "creation" of new animals. Fetal tissue research holds out the promise of help for diabetics and those with Parkinson's disease, but even using the tissue, quite apart from how we acquire it, is a controversial affair. Equally contentious is the bringing to term of severely deformed fetuses who will die almost at once, in order to use their organs for transplant. But, so, too, is xenography, or cross-species transplantation, in which animals are treated as repositories of organs for humans.

Social, political, and legal decisions always spur ethical interest. Topics such as obscenity, pornography, and censorship are of perennial interest, as are straightforwardly economic/political issues to do with capital punishment, equality, majoritarian democracy, the moral assessment of capitalism, and the provision of societal welfare. Today, some comparatively new issues have come to figure in this ethical landscape, from the place of children in society and all manner of interest in educational policy and practice to population policy and the relation of this to the distribution of various societal resources. And it is obvious that, throughout the world, issues to do with nationalism, political and judicial sovereignty, and immigration are of massive interest to educated persons and raise all kinds of moral questions.

This new series, For and Against, aims to cover a good many of these applied issues. Collectively, the volumes will form a kind of library of applied ethics.

Philosophy is an argumentative discipline: Among its best practitioners, whom this series will feature, it proceeds by the clear and careful articulation, analysis, and assessment of arguments. Clashes of arguments, ideas, principles, positions, and theories are its very lifeblood. The idea behind the series is very simple: It is to capture this clash. Two or more philosophers, in opposition on some moral, social, or political issue, will state and defend their positions on the issue in as direct and powerful a manner as they can. Theory will be involved, but the general aim is not to have two authors differ over the development or worth of a philosophical theory. Rather, it is to show the application of philosophy to practice, with each author using as much theory as he or she thinks necessary to state and defend his or her position on the topic. Educated people generally should be able to read and assess the success of the authors.

The volumes will be polemical but in the best sense: Each author will dispute and defend a position on some controversial matter by means of clear and careful argument. The end, obviously, is that each volume will exhibit to the full the best case each author can muster for his or her respective side to the controversy.

We are, it is sometimes said today, involved in a "war on drugs." Whole communities, including the most vulnerable segments of them, are held to be battlegrounds of this war, and our prison populations have grown as drug offenses are prosecuted with vigor. How are we to conduct this "war"? What are we to do about the growing number of drug offenders who swell our prisons? What steps ought we take to deal with the reality of drugs in our midst? The present volume takes up the very controversial and politically contentious matter of whether drugs should be legalized. Once certain conceptual issues are clarified, and once certain empirical matters are sorted out, Douglas Husak, a distinguished philosopher of law, argues in favor of legalization while Peter de Marneffe, a distinguished political philosopher, argues against it. Which drugs are involved, which drugs should be legalized, and how drug offenses should be regarded all figure in this discussion, as do issues involving soft drugs as the precursors of hard ones and the relationship of drug taking and crime. It should be possible for readers at the end of the discussion to understand the social/political issues involved, to have at least some grasp of the empirical questions that bear upon the debate, and to appreciate the clashing arguments by which each side hopes to buttress its case. As will become evident, the debate is spirited, but it is conducted in a clear and careful prose that should enable readers to decide for themselves where they stand on legalization.

R. G. Frey

The Legalization of Drugs

I For Drug Legalization

Douglas Husak

1   The Meaning of Drug Decriminalization

PHILOSOPHERS are good at clarifying issues. The initial issue I propose to debate is whether drugs should be *criminalized* or *decriminalized*. This issue needs to be clarified. In principle, the ideas of drug criminalization and drug decriminalization are straightforward. Anyone who proposes that a given drug should be *criminalized* means simply that *the use of that drug should be a criminal offense*. By contrast, those who favor *decriminalization* mean simply that *the use of that drug should not be a criminal offense*.

As the issue is so defined, it is fairly easy to understand why some citizens are *for* drug decriminalization and others are *against* it. What is harder to fathom is why the idea of decriminalization itself is so difficult to grasp. Admittedly, commentators on both sides of this debate have contributed to the confusion by using terms like *criminalize* and *decriminalize* in different and inconsistent ways.[1] Sometimes, they have used the term *decriminalize* interchangeably with *legalize*. Of course, people are free to use these words however they like, as long as they are careful to explain what they mean. Here, I use the term *drug legalization* to refer to a system in which the *production* and *sale* of drugs are not criminal offenses. In my judgment, decriminalization is a much more basic issue than legalization. We should not try to decide what the law

1 Decriminalization is sometimes defined to include a *reduction* in the severity of criminal punishments. See, for example, Robert J. MacCoun and Peter Reuter, *Drug War Heresies* (Cambridge: Cambridge University Press, 2001), p. 40. As the term is so defined, finding a commentator who does not endorse drug decriminalization is nearly impossible.

should say about drug production and sale unless we are clear about what the law should say about drug use. Thus I propose to begin with a discussion of decriminalization and not proceed to an examination of legalization until Chapter 5.

In this first of five chapters, I will try to clarify the meaning of drug decriminalization. I anticipate that readers who are already reasonably knowledgeable about the topic will be eager to move directly to the arguments that constitute the bulk of my half of this volume. In the following chapters – and in Chapters 3 and 4 in particular – I will attempt to persuade readers to endorse my proposal to decriminalize drugs. But we must be patient. I am confident that a great ideal of resistance to my position rests on a misunderstanding of exactly what I am (and am not) proposing. If I am correct, this preliminary chapter is absolutely crucial if we want to ensure that we are all talking about the same thing when we debate whether or not to decriminalize drugs.

This chapter consists of three sections, each of which addresses confusions about the meaning of drug decriminalization. The first section focuses on the meaning of *decriminalization*; the second discusses what is meant when a substance is said to be a *drug;* and the third examines whether proposals to criminalize or de-criminalize a particular drug must be sensitive to the *purpose* for which that drug is used. Each of these matters turns out to be surprisingly complex.

Decriminalization

Let us begin by asking exactly what is meant when we say that the use of a drug is (or is not) a criminal offense. Conduct (such as the use of a drug) is made a criminal offense when legisla-tors *prohibit* that conduct by enacting a statute that subjects per-sons who engage in it to *punishment*. In other words, the use of a given drug is criminalized if and only if people become eligible for punishment for using that drug. Of course, to say that people become *subject* to or *eligible* for punishment does not imply that they *will* be punished. Most people who break criminal laws are never caught, arrested, prosecuted, convicted, or punished. But this fact is beside the point I am making here, which is about the *meaning* of criminal offense. The state cannot punish people unless they have committed a crime – a criminal offense. Anyone who proposes that a given drug should be *decriminalized* means that *the state should not punish people simply for using that drug*.

Unfortunately, what I have said thus far only begins to clarify the issue, since confusion about the meaning of decriminalization simply reappears at a new and deeper level. Suppose legislatures enact statutes that allow the state to respond to drug users in various ways. If we are uncertain about whether any of these state responses is a kind of *punishment*, we will be uncertain about whether drug use has been criminalized or decriminalized. In most cases, we are not at all confused about this matter. If legislators draft statutes that allow the state to sentence persons who use a drug to prison, we have no doubt that the use of that drug has been made a crime. Sometimes, however, we *are* uncertain about whether state responses are a kind of punishment. When we are unclear about this, we should also be unclear about whether what that person has done is or is not a crime.

I mention our uncertainty about whether some kinds of state responses amount to kinds of punishments because it complicates our understanding of the meaning of decriminalization generally, and of drug decriminalization in particular. Drug decriminalization, as I define it here, means that drug use is not a crime. If drug use is not a crime, people cannot be punished for using drugs. But what kinds of state responses to drug users are kinds of punishments, and therefore ruled out by decriminalization? Suppose, for example, that the police write tickets to people they detect using a drug such as marijuana. These tickets, let us further suppose, are paid by a monetary fine, much as parking tickets are. Those who are ticketed have the option to plead guilty and pay their fine through the mail or contest the charge and go to trial. If they go to trial and lose, their fine will almost always be greater than what they would have paid if they had pled guilty. If they fail to pay this fine, they will be sentenced to jail. Does the system I have just described amount to the decriminalization of marijuana? The answer is unclear, and I will not attempt to resolve it here. The important point is that if this system *punishes* users of marijuana, then marijuana has *not* been decriminalized. But if this system does *not* punish users of marijuana, then marijuana *has* been decriminalized.

This debate about what kinds of state responses to drug users are kinds of punishments is important when well-intentioned reformers, dissatisfied with our current policy, propose that drug users should be required to undergo *treatment* instead of being sent to jail. The movement to treat rather than to imprison drug users continues to gain momentum. Consider, for example, Proposition 36, approved by a 3 to 2 margin by California voters in 2000. This proposition requires many individuals caught using illicit drugs to subject themselves to treatment. Failure to undergo treatment, or to undergo treatment successfully, subjects the drug user to jail. The trend toward treating drug users instead of imprisoning them is not peculiar to California. Throughout the United States today, somewhere between 1 million and 1.5 million Americans are coerced into 12-step alcohol and drug treatment programs each year, often because they "choose" to participate rather than endure some other hardship.[2] Treatment is an option some states offer as a way to avoid imprisonment for, say, drunk driving. Such proposals are generally regarded as humane and cost-effective alternatives to punishment. Sponsors of Proposition 36 argued that 36,000 fewer people would be imprisoned each year simply for possessing illicit drugs.

Do these proposals amount to drug decriminalization? The answer is not obvious. I am inclined to believe that mandatory treatment is *not* an alternative to punishment; it is simply a different *kind* of punishment. If I am correct, support for decriminalization is incompatible with support for treatment as a forced alternative to jail. No one who favors decriminalization can approve of mandatory drug treatment, unless he or she believes that coerced treatment is not a kind of punishment. Decriminalization does not allow the state to sentence drug users to treatment any more than

---

2 See Stanton Peele and Charles Bufe with Archie Brodsky, *Resisting 12-Step Coercion* (Tucson, AZ: Sharp Press, 2000).

it allows the state to sentence drug users to jail. I have little doubt that treatment is preferable to incarceration if we must choose between the two. But we need not make this choice. We need not assume that drug users must be either bad – and deserve punishment – or sick – and in need of treatment whether they like it or not. We have a third option. Our criminal justice system might leave people alone when they merely use a drug. If we choose this latter option, we might say that the state allows people to be *free* to use drugs. If people are truly free to use drugs, there can be no doubt that the state has decriminalized drug use.

Uncertainties about whether an activity has been criminalized can be drawn from familiar examples in which activities are licensed. Is it a crime to drive a car or to practice medicine? The answer, of course, is that these activities are crimes unless persons have a license. Suppose we decided to license drug users. Would such a system amount to decriminalization? It is hard to say. Perhaps our answer should depend on how difficult it is to obtain a license. Suppose we implement a system of "heroin maintenance," which allows users to take heroin without fear of criminal penalties at licensed facilities. Would this system amount to decriminalization? At some point, we should recognize that the contrast between criminalization and decriminalization is simplistic, obscuring the full range of alternatives that are available to regulate drug use.

Confusion about whether a proposal is a form of criminalization or decriminalization is rampant. Frequently, reformers are deliberately evasive about this issue. Sometimes officials talk about such concepts as "bans" or "prohibitions" without being clear about whether they are talking about criminal laws that subject people to punishments. In 2003, for example, Surgeon General Richard Carmona explicitly expressed his support for the banning of tobacco products – the first time a surgeon general had made such a recommendation. When testifying before a House Energy and Commerce subcommittee, Carmona affirmed that he would "support the abolition of all tobacco products." He declined to say whether he favored a specific law to ban tobacco, indicating that "legislation is not my field." He did, however, affirm that he "would support banning or abolishing tobacco products."

How should we understand Carmona's proposal? It is hard to see how tobacco products could be "abolished." What *could* be done, however, is to *criminalize* tobacco use – to make smoking (or otherwise using) tobacco products a criminal offense. This proposal threatens to punish the tens of millions of Americans who currently smoke tobacco. I do not believe for a moment that this would be a good idea, but that is not my point. My point is that we need to be clear about exactly *what* is being proposed. If Carmona's plea to "ban" or "abolish" tobacco products involves subjecting smokers to punishments, it is reasonable to expect him to say so.

Confusion about the meaning of proposals to decriminalize some illicit drugs such as marijuana is prominent as well. Between 1973 and 1978, 11 states are said to have "decriminalized" the possession of small amounts of marijuana: Alaska, California, Colorado, Maine, Minnesota, Mississippi, Nebraska, New York, North Carolina, Ohio, and Oregon. Alaska has since tried to re-criminalize, and Oregon has decriminalized after recriminalizing. Several cities and counties also passed laws that were said to amount to decriminalization. But these states and cities respond to drug users in very different ways, making it unclear what "decriminalization" really means. In some of these places, possession results in the loss of a driver's license for 90 days. If this response amounts to a kind of punishment, we should not conclude that these jurisdictions have implemented a policy of marijuana decriminalization as I define it here.

Proposals in neighboring countries are no more clear. In 2002, the Canadian Senate issued a voluminous report that urged Parliament to "legalize" marijuana. In response, the Chretien government introduced a bill to "decriminalize" the possession of a half-ounce. The amount to be decriminalized was reduced from a full ounce after Attorney General John Ashcroft and the drug czar, John Walters, made threats to slow traffic at the Canadian border. Some newspaper editorials characterized this plan to "decriminalize" marijuana as a "one-word lie." The proposed policy would allow the police to give tickets to citizens caught with half an ounce. The bill would not grant Canadians the freedom to use marijuana. Only the mode of punishment would be changed.

Despite these uncertainties, I regard confusion about whether drug users may be given tickets or required to undergo treatment as relatively minor details that should not obscure what is crystal clear about decriminalization. What is beyond controversy is that a sentence of jail for drug use is a punishment for a crime. Therefore, no one can endorse decriminalization unless he or she agrees that drug users should not be sent to jail or prison. This is the core idea of decriminalization I will presuppose throughout the remainder of this book. But confusion about the meaning of decriminalization persists, even if we stick to this core idea. In what follows, I will describe several things that drug decriminalization is *not*. We can better appreciate what decriminalization means when we avoid the various ways it is misunderstood.

In the first place, decriminalization only pertains to punitive state policies toward drug *users*. It is noncommittal about how illicit drugs should be produced or sold. Those who support decriminalization may believe that no one should be allowed to manufacture or distribute illicit drugs. Most defenders of decriminalization would probably be unhappy about a policy that punished producers or distributors of drugs. I will return to this important topic of legalization in Chapter 5. But decriminalization *itself* implies no position on these issues. Decriminalization says only that users themselves should not be punished. What happens to *other* participants in the drug trade remains an open question, to be decided only after we are clear what the criminal justice system should do about users.

Because decriminalization itself says nothing about producers or sellers of drugs, we should not regard decriminalization as a comprehensive drug policy. In other words, those who favor decriminalization should not be understood to offer a "solution" to our country's "drug problem." Those who advocate decriminalization may propose any number of imaginative solutions or believe that the problem has no solution at all. They may (and do) differ greatly among themselves about what an "ideal drug policy" would look like. Their only point of agreement is that punishing drug users should not be an acceptable part of that policy.

In addition, those who favor decriminalization need not believe that drug use should be approved or condoned by the state. The contrary supposition has been a major obstacle to understanding decriminalization. Many people reject decriminalization because they fear it "sends the wrong message" about drug use. According to this train of thought, decriminalization sends the message that drug use is permissible; that drug use is not wrong. But decriminalization itself takes no position on whether drug use is wrong. Many activities that should not be subjected to punishment are wrong. We can all describe any number of activities – such as breaking our promises or lying to our friends – that no one proposes to criminalize, even though almost everyone agrees that they are wrong. Similarly, decriminalization does not imply that we condone or approve of drug use. In no other context do we think that the failure to punish people indicates that we condone or approve of what they do. To be antiprohibition is not to be pro-drug.

In case there is doubt, notice that support for decriminalization is consistent with any number of state strategies designed to discourage drug use – as long as these strategies are not kinds of punishments. The state may try to influence behavior through taxation and education. We can produce less of whatever behavior we do not want by taxing it heavily or by educating people about its dangers. Schools might test students for illicit drugs and sanction them in various ways if their test results are positive. Possible sanctions might include not allowing drug users to participate in extracurricular activities – a sanction allowed by the Supreme Court in 2003. A host of additional strategies to shape behavior are available to the state as well. The Office of National Drug Control Policy has encouraged major movie studios to promote antidrug messages in their films. The office has made agreements with Internet search engine companies so that antidrug advertisements automatically appear on the computer screens of persons who search for such terms as *pot* and *weed*. Drug reform

ads, including those favoring medical marijuana, might be prohibited as well. As long as these kinds of efforts are made, no one
should be tempted to think that the state condones or approves
of drug use, even if it does not resort to punishments.

A variety of responses by the private sector might be extraordinarily effective in discouraging the use of illicit drugs and are
compatible with decriminalization. Let me mention a few. I do
not endorse any of these ideas as desirable; my only point is that
they are not ruled out by decriminalization as I define it here.
Private employers might test employees for drugs, and even fire
those who fail the tests. Landlords might be allowed to require
tenants to abstain from given drugs specified in a lease and to
evict those who violate their agreements. Clubs like the Kiwanis
Club and organizations like the Girl Scouts need not implement
a policy of nondiscrimination against drug users. Needless to say,
these examples are not imaginary; 196 of the Fortune 200 companies require preemployment or random drug tests. Of course, all
of these sanctions are precluded by decriminalization if they are
modes of state punishment. But I do not believe that people are
punished by the state when they are barred from private clubs,
fired from their jobs, or evicted from their apartments. These consequences are hardships or deprivations – sometimes more severe
than the effects of being thrown into jail – but I do not regard them
as kinds of punishments. If I am correct, these kinds of responses
to drug use are compatible with decriminalization as I understand
it here.

In addition, it is crucial to realize that decriminalization allows
the state to criminalize drug use in specific contexts in which it
is especially dangerous. Although a state that has decriminalized
drugs may not punish drug use per se, it may punish persons who
increase various tangible risks by using drugs. The clearest example is driving under the influence of drugs that impair judgment
or performance. All states prohibit drunk driving, even though
no state criminalizes alcohol use itself. In order to be punished,
persons must combine drug use with some other activity that
is particularly risky. The criminal offense, then, is not drug use
per se, but drug use while performing the risky activity. Of course,

driving is not the only activity that persons might be punished for performing while under the influence of a drug that impairs judgment or performance. Similar prohibitions might apply to people who operate heavy machinery, fly airplanes, perform surgery, fire guns, and the like. These activities are dangerous even when undertaken by persons whose faculties are intact. When judgment or performance is impaired by drug use, these activities become too dangerous to tolerate. Decriminalization would allow persons who engage in these dangerous acts to be punished.

Thus the criminal law need not be indifferent about drugs, even without punishing drug use itself. One controversial proposal is to treat drug use as an aggravating factor in sentencing persons for nondrug offenses. In other words, murderers and rapists, for example, might be punished more severely if they commit their crimes under the influence of drugs. Once again, I do not mention this possibility in order to defend it, but only to indicate its compatibility with decriminalization as I understand it here. I need hardly say that decriminalization has no implications for whether individuals will come to regard illicit drug use as fashionable and trendy, or as foolish and reprehensible. The general point should now be clear. Decriminalization is not a formula for how society at large should think about illicit drug users. Individuals and institutions might continue to respond negatively to drug use – with one important limitation. A state that has decriminalized drugs will not allow drug users to be punished.

Decriminalization – not punishing drug users – can be brought about in either of two ways. We might distinguish between what are called de jure and de facto decriminalization. Under de jure decriminalization, all existing crimes of illicit drug use will be repealed. These statutes would be removed from the books by a deliberate legislative act. Under de facto decriminalization, these crimes will no longer be enforced. They will continue to exist as anachronisms, comparable to laws prohibiting sodomy or adultery. As a matter of fact, no one will be arrested, prosecuted, convicted, or punished for violating these laws. We should probably prefer the explicit repeal of crimes of drug use to the alternative of de facto criminalization. Laws that still exist can be enforced occasionally and selectively. Even sporadic enforcement of these laws is incompatible with decriminalization. Nonetheless, de facto decriminalization would be far easier to implement. Our society does not really know how to conduct a debate about whether a law should be repealed, and the attempt to do so is likely to galvanize support in its favor. In fact, few criminal laws are ever repealed. We readily add new criminal laws to our codes but rarely remove them. Outdated criminal laws are much more likely to fall into disuse than to be repealed directly. It is less politically controversial simply to stop enforcing these laws than actually to require the legislature to remove them from our criminal codes. As long as people are not arrested or punished for using drugs, we should not be very concerned about whether this result is achieved through de jure or de facto decriminalization.

Finally, we can be *selective* about criminalization. To this point, I have pretended that the debate is about whether or not to decriminalize "drugs," without further distinctions among the several different kinds of drugs we may want to decriminalize. But we might decriminalize some but not all drugs. In all probability, the case for criminalization should proceed on a drug-by-drug basis. Each drug has different effects on individual users and on society generally. If we want to proceed cautiously, marijuana is the sensible place to begin. Marijuana is the most widely used and least dangerous illicit drug; the arguments for criminalization I will evaluate in Chapter 3 are least plausible when applied to this case. My own preference is more bold – I am not persuaded that we have good enough reasons to punish those who use *any* drug. We can easily *imagine* a hypothetical drug that we would want to criminalize, but the rationales I will explore do not seem sufficiently compelling to justify criminalizing any drug that actually exists.

Still, I readily admit that arguments for prohibition are more plausible for some drugs than for others. But we cannot decide which drugs to prohibit without first attending to rationales for criminalization. We must know *what* would count as a good reason to prohibit a drug before we can decide *which* drugs to prohibit. Thus our work is not complete when we divide existing drugs into two categories: those we will criminalize and those we will decriminalize. We should not be satisfied when we have decided, for example, that caffeine and tobacco should be placed into the latter category, whereas heroin and cocaine should be assigned to the former category. We need to develop *criteria* for making these classifications. These criteria are needed for two reasons. First, our drug policy must be *principled*; we need to know *why* we categorize drugs as we do. Second, laboratories are certain to create new drugs that people will want to use. These drugs will have to be assigned to one category or the other. We should not simply assume that all of these new drugs must be prohibited. In this vein, consider a warning cast by William Bennett. He cautions: "New illegal products will no doubt continue to appear. . . . Whichever happens to be the drug of the day, our job is to persist in making it difficult to buy, sell, or use it." But "new" drugs are not "illegal" when they "appear." They only become illegal when legislators decide to prohibit them. Why should we assume that those who use the new "drug of the day" must be punished? It is not hard to imagine a new drug that society should condone and even welcome.

Drugs

The last of the preceding observations makes a natural transition to my second topic. Uncertainties about words like *criminalize* and *decriminalize* represent only part of the difficulty in attempts to understand the meaning of drug decriminalization. Enormous confusion also surrounds the nature of *drugs*. In inviting readers to consider different policies for different drugs, we cannot fail to notice that different policies for different drugs *already* exist. Criminalization has always been *selective*. We do not punish adult users of alcohol or tobacco, and caffeine is permitted even for children. Are these substances really drugs?

Unfortunately, no entirely satisfactory definition of a drug exists. Let us examine the definition most frequently contained in those statutes that prohibit drugs: "any substance other than food which by its chemical nature affects the structure or function of the living organism." What is noteworthy about this definition is what it does *not* contain. It does not purport to use *the law* to distinguish substances that are drugs from substances that are not drugs. This definition makes no mention of the law at all. For this reason, this definition deviates from the way ordinary speakers of English tend to identify drugs. Empirical studies indicate that respondents are far more likely to classify a substance as a drug when its use is prohibited. Relatively few Americans regard alcohol, tobacco, or caffeine as a drug, whereas nearly everyone recognizes heroin, cocaine, and marijuana as drugs. Politicians, in addition to the public, commonly use the law to decide whether or not a substance is a drug. But nothing in the definition of a drug provides any reason to exempt alcohol, tobacco, and caffeine from the scope of a comprehensive drug policy. Unquestionably, according to the definition I have cited, alcohol, tobacco, and caffeine *are* drugs. There is absolutely no pharmacological basis for questioning the classification of these substances as drugs. We should say that these substances are *licit* drugs.

Surely the question of whether a given substance is a drug should depend on its pharmacological properties and its effects on persons who use it, rather than on how or whether it is regulated by law. The status of a substance as a drug should not fluctuate as legal regulations are enacted and repealed. Opiates and cocaine were not suddenly transformed from nondrugs into drugs in the early part of the 20th century, when the state first began to punish people for using them.[3] Moreover, if we decide to allow people to use a drug, it does not magically become something other than a drug at the moment its use is permitted. U.S. Food and Drug Administration (FDA) approval does not transform drugs into nondrugs. Most importantly, the whole point of this book is to question whether our drug policy is just. Surely this inquiry is sensible, even if my arguments turn out to be unpersuasive. We should not prevent our conclusions about drug policy from being

3 Perhaps the best history of illicit drugs is David F. Musto, *The American Disease: Origins of Narcotic Control*, 3d ed. (New York: Oxford University Press, 1999).

applied to licit substances simply because we have defined them as something other than drugs.

Nonetheless, the foregoing definition is problematic. It is too broad – and not just because it includes alcohol, tobacco, and caffeine. Many very familiar substances seem to qualify as drugs according to this definition, even though no one would think to classify them as drugs. Consider water or salt. Surely water and salt are substances. Surely they affect the structure or function of living people. Surely their effects are caused by chemical processes. If there is anything in the definition that shows these substances not to be drugs, it must be that salt and water are foods. Are salt and water foods? Why can't a substance be both a drug and a food? What exactly is a food? Is a food any ingested substance that people cannot live without? People cannot live without some amount of metal in their body. Are these metals therefore foods? Surely not. Are they drugs? That, too, seems doubtful. But why not? What in the definition rules out this (presumably absurd) result? In light of these (and other) difficulties, this definition is inadequate. Unless a better candidate becomes available, it is fair to conclude that no satisfactory definition of a drug exists. When we purport to be talking about drugs, it is doubtful that we know what it is we are talking about.

The difficulty of deciding whether given substances qualify as drugs has emerged as a major problem in public health. Any "health food store" contains a great number of substances that are alleged to be effective in treating various ailments and deficiencies. The manufacture and distribution of these substances often escape regulation altogether – with grave health consequences to persons who use them. These substances often (but not always) are said to be "herbs" or "herbal remedies." Are herbs drugs? If not, is marijuana a drug? Return to the preceding definition. As for water and salt, the only possible basis for disqualifying herbs as drugs is that herbs are foods. Are herbs foods? Can they be both foods and drugs? Are they neither foods nor drugs?

Our best definition of drugs is not very helpful in answering these straightforward questions. We do not really have a good idea of what a drug is. The plain fact is that, in many cases, we have no clear means to decide whether a given substance is or is not a drug. If we do not know exactly what a drug is, we may be unable to construct anything that deserves to be called a *drug policy*. Arguably, we will not make progress in the debate about drug decriminalization if we retain a concept – the concept of a drug – that we do not understand. Perhaps we should abandon this concept altogether.

The proposal to abandon the concept of a drug should be taken seriously. After all, what reasons do we have to want a policy that pertains exclusively to drugs? Suppose we become persuaded that substantial risks to public health are posed by the use of a food or an herbal remedy. Why should the question of whether or how we should regulate these substances depend on whether we classify them as *drugs*? We should enact whatever regulations are sensible, however we ultimately decide to categorize the substances we regulate. We can accomplish all of our regulatory objectives without employing the concept of a drug at all.

The proposal to abandon the concept of a drug is radical – probably *too* radical. The concept of a drug is too entrenched in our discourse to be removed. Nor is it clear what concept we should substitute in its place. Therefore, despite my misgivings, I will continue to suppose that our debate is about *drugs*. I will pretend that the preceding definition is adequate, and that we are able to apply it to nearly any substance to decide whether or not that substance is a drug. I will assume that the question of whether a given substance is or is not a drug is important for public policy.

Recreational Use

One final matter needs to be clarified. Thus far, I have indicated that the question to be raised is whether or not drugs should be decriminalized. But expressing the issue in this way is simplistic and misleading. Arguably, we cannot decide whether to criminalize or decriminalize drug use without specifying the *purpose* for which that drug is used. If so, our topic is not really about drug use per se, but rather about a particular *kind* of drug use – that is, a particular *reason* for using drugs. We might well decide that one and the same drug – cocaine, morphine, or Prozac – should be decriminalized for some purposes, but criminalized for others. Presumably, the use of these drugs should not be a criminal offense when people have a *medical* reason to take them. No one has qualms about entering a drug store to purchase a substance (available by prescription or otherwise) for a medical purpose. But attitudes, reactions, and state policy might be entirely different when that same drug is used for a nonmedical purpose. In many cases, the state punishes persons who use that drug without a medical need.

The distinction between medical and nonmedical drug use is absolutely crucial if we hope to understand our present drug policy and replace it with something better. Since this distinction is so important, it invites further scrutiny. Although drugs can be used for several different kinds of nonmedical purposes, one such purpose is especially significant. This use is *recreational*. It is hard to be precise in characterizing when use is recreational. Roughly, people engage in recreational activities – whether or not these activities involve a drug – in order to seek pleasure, euphoria, satisfaction, or some other positive psychological state. When a drug is used in order to attain a positive psychological state – a drug *high* – I will call that use *recreational*.

The contrast between medical and recreational drug use is *not* a contrast between two kinds of drugs. Again, one and the same drug might be used for either a medical or a recreational purpose. Therefore, the term *recreational drug* is potentially misleading. Since just about any drug might be used for a recreational purpose, a recreational drug can only be a drug that is *typically* or *generally* used for a recreational purpose. Alcohol is one such drug. Marijuana is another. But since these drugs can be (and are) used nonrecreationally, we should be reluctant to classify them as "recreational drugs." Instead, we should classify them as drugs with a predominant recreational *use*. To be precise, we should always use the adverbial form of the word *recreational*. The word modifies the verb *use*, as in "to use recreationally," rather than the noun *drug*, as in "recreational drug." I will not always be so precise; the term *recreational drug* is simpler than *drug used recreationally*. But we must be careful not to be misled by this imprecision.

Under our present policy, the response of the state toward drug users depends on the purpose for which the drug is used. A recreational user of a given drug may face severe punishment; nothing at all is done to that same person when his or her use of that drug is medical. Since this distinction is so important, one would hope that the line between medical and recreational purposes would be fairly clear. We need to know, *When are drugs used medically, and when are drugs used recreationally?* If the contrast between medical and recreational use proves very hard to draw, we can anticipate that the response of the state – which depends on this contrast – will prove difficult to justify.

When *are* drugs used medically? The most popular drugs can be used to illustrate the difficulty of answering this question. Consider caffeine – and try to decide when it is used medically, as opposed to when is it used recreationally. Why do people drink caffeine? Why do people typically prefer regular coffee, and why do they occasionally choose coffee that is decaffeinated? The obvious answer is that people tend to use caffeine when they want to attain a given psychological state – when they want to become more alert, awake, or energetic. Should we categorize this purpose as recreational? Perhaps – although I think that the question is hard. Suppose a student drinks coffee in the morning to combat drowsiness. Is this use medical or recreational? Fortunately, we do not *need* to answer this question. Caffeine is among those drugs permitted either for medical or for recreational purposes. But the distinction between recreational and medical use becomes important when we consider other drugs as examples. Suppose the student substitutes amphetamines for caffeine. Is this use recreational or medical? We have asked the same question as before, but here it is crucial, since state policy differs depending on how we answer it. If his use is recreational, he is a criminal; if his use is medical, he is not. How do we decide which answer is correct?

Generally, drugs are used for a medical rather than for a recreational purpose when they are used to treat a medical

condition – a *disease* or *illnesses*. With this answer in mind, return to the drowsy student who uses caffeine or Dexedrin. We
are now in a better position to understand whether his use of
these drugs is recreational or medical. His drug use is medical if it
is taken to treat a disease or illness. If we cannot decide whether
the student suffers from a disease or illness, we will be unable
to decide whether his drug use is medical. *Does* the drowsiness
of our student qualify as a disease or illness? Some think so. In
2003, the United States Army tested an antisleep agent called
modafinil. Sold under the name Provigil, this compound can keep
users awake for two or three days at a stretch. But modafinil is
not just for soldiers. This same year, the FDA was asked to allow
physicians to prescribe Provigil for lesser sleep problems, such as
shift-work drowsiness. Even without that approval, the drug is
attracting a wider market. Truck drivers and students account for
a growing portion of Provigil's $200 million in annual sales.

Whether drowsiness is *really* a disease cannot be answered
without a theory, or a criterion, to distinguish those conditions
that are diseases or illnesses from those that are not. We can evade
this question by trusting doctors to draw this distinction. But we
need to have some general understanding of how doctors do what
we trust them to do. On what basis do they decide whether the
drowsiness of the student is a disease or illness? In many cases,
the determination that a condition is a disease is obvious and beyond controversy. No one challenges the classification of cancer
as a disease. In a growing number of cases, however, we cannot
provide a satisfactory answer to this question. If the contrast is
nearly impossible to draw, the state policy that depends on this
contrast will be nearly impossible to justify.

The line between conditions that are diseases or illnesses and
those that are not – and the corresponding distinction between
medical and recreational drug use – has always been tenuous
and is becoming more difficult to draw every day. The difficulty is
compounded because drugs are no longer prescribed only for the
treatment of a disease or illness. The conditions for which drugs
are prescribed now include *syndromes* and *disorders*. Our confidence in our ability to recognize a medical condition when we

see one evaporates in the face of the growing number of syndromes and disorders that are recognized today. What exactly *is* a
syndrome or disorder? Many commentators have noted that we
live in an era in which problems tend to be *medicalized*. That is,
every problem is conceptualized as a medical condition, eligible
to be treated with drugs. The phenomenon of medicalization is
most pervasive in the United States, which leads the world in the
consumption of licit drugs to change mood and behavior. Sexual
conditions – and drugs used to treat these conditions – illustrate
this phenomenon. Consider Viagra, for example. Does the inability to maintain an erection really qualify as a medical condition –
the disease or syndrome of erectile dysfunction? How should we
decide? After all, the condition this drug treats has little to do
with reproduction and everything to do with sexual pleasure.
Viagra is used largely by men who are beyond the age at which
they want to reproduce; it is taken for purposes that seemingly
qualify as recreational rather than medical. At the very least, this
drug illustrates the extreme difficulty of drawing the line between
medical and recreational drug use.

The inability to maintain an erection during sex is hardly the
only sexual condition that is hard to categorize as a disease, illness,
syndrome, or disorder. Countless other examples could be given.
Does the failure to attain an orgasm during sexual intercourse
qualify as a medical condition? Would we classify as medical a
drug that increased the joy of sex by producing more intense
orgasms? Or by producing multiple orgasms? What would we
say about a drug that produced orgasms by direct stimulation
of the brain, without requiring sex at all? How do we decide to
answer these questions? What arguments should we make to try
to persuade someone who disagreed with our answers?

Sex is not the only context in which the contrast between medical and recreational drug use becomes fuzzy. If a drug qualifies as
medical when used to enhance sexual passion, what should we
say about a drug that enhances the pleasure of other activities –
such as eating, watching movies, or listening to music? Would a
substance that relieved the boredom of housework such as laun-
dry and dishwashing have a medical use as well? How should we

categorize drugs used for the many "eating disorders" that now are recognized? Someone who eats too fast, experiences guilt over eating too much, eats when not hungry, or is heavier than he or she would like may suffer from "binge eating disorder" – a condition for which antidepressants may be prescribed. Are these drugs used medically? These questions are important, because people who use these same drugs for recreational purposes can be sent to prison. Some of the questions I have asked are fanciful at the present time. But there is no reason to believe that pharmaceutical companies are incapable of creating substances that add to the pleasure of everyday tasks or help us to attain the kind of body shape we desire. If existing drugs do not demonstrate the difficulties of drawing the line between recreational and medical use, we can be sure that new drugs are on the horizon that will blur that line to the vanishing point.

Of course, many of the questions I have raised are *not* fanciful. Consider new substances such as Celebrex. Advertisements promise that Celebrex "can make you feel like you again." Celebrex is said to be "not for everyone," and prospective users are encouraged to ask their doctors whether Celebrex is "right for you." Other pills are marketed to bring about something called "enhancement" or to "take off the sharp edges." Clearly, such substances illustrate the difficulty of contrasting medical and recreational drug use. Many people use ecstasy for the same reason they use Viagra – to enhance their sexual pleasure. They use cocaine for the same reason they use caffeine – to remain alert. They use marijuana for the same reason they use amphetamines – to overcome the tedium of routine, everyday tasks. At the present time, doctors are not permitted to prescribe most of these drugs because they are said to have no medical use. I have tried to raise doubts about how to understand the elusive concept of "medical use." Without a better theory of disease or illness, it is impossible to decide when a drug is used medically as opposed to recreationally.

When a distinction proves virtually impossible to draw, we should review our reasons for trying to draw it. Why should it really *matter* whether a drug is used for a medical or a recreational purpose? As I have indicated, our present drug policy attaches extraordinary significance to this distinction. Persons who use opiates medically are left alone; persons who use them recreationally can be punished. Eventually, of course, I want to assess and evaluate our drug policy, not merely describe it. *Why* should our policy place such enormous weight on the distinction between medical and recreational use? What is there about recreational drug use, as opposed to medical drug use, that could possibly justify a punitive state response?

Ultimately, I do not believe that a satisfactory answer can be given. The distinction between recreational and medical use, which has proved so hard to draw, is probably not worth preserving as a cornerstone of our drug policy. In other words, this distinction cannot bear the great weight that our existing policy has placed upon it. Obviously, those who support our present drug policy do not agree. They continue to apply totally different regulations to drugs used for a medical purpose than to drugs used for a recreational purpose – even for the same drug.

I fear that my efforts to clarify the topic of drug decriminalization have confused the issue more than they have illuminated it. I began by asking what criminalization and decriminalization mean and concluded that the answer is murky because we are not totally sure about whether given kinds of state responses to drug users are modes of punishments. Next, I expressed doubts about whether we have a precise definition of a drug. Arguably, we cannot decide whether drugs should be criminalized or decriminalized unless we know what drugs are. Finally, I introduced the fundamental distinction between recreational and medical drug use. Unfortunately, it is far from obvious when a drug is used recreationally, and when it is used medically. Although it seems clear that a drug is used medically when it is taken in the treatment of a disease or illness, we lack a good theory of when a condition qualifies as a disease or illness.

In light of these problems, we may have legitimate reservations about whether our topic is sufficiently precise to allow us to proceed. Despite my fears, I believe that some progress can be made. We will debate whether the recreational use of particular drugs such as alcohol, marijuana, tobacco, cocaine, heroin, and ecstasy should or should not be a criminal offense. Our current policy punishes recreational users of many but not all of these drugs. Is this policy defensible? Ultimately, this is the issue I propose to address. Before examining it directly, however, we must discuss yet another preliminary matter. We must decide how we will know when one answer is better than another. That is, we must identify the criteria that need to be satisfied before we should be persuaded to prefer drug criminalization to decriminalization. I now turn to this difficult issue.

2   How Should We Evaluate
Alternative Drug Policies?

T HE issue, then – albeit somewhat less clear than we would like – is whether or not the state should punish people simply for using drugs for recreational purposes. How should we decide what position to take on this issue? More generally, how should we evaluate the many possible ideas about how our drug policy might be reformed? All philosophers believe that progress is made by assessing arguments. But first we must decide what to argue *about*. As a society, we really do not know how to conduct a public debate about criminal laws generally and about drug offenses in particular.

We cannot hope to make progress on any topic unless we begin by asking the right question. In the present context, that question is, *Should drug use be criminalized?* A different version of this same question is, *Should persons be punished simply for using drugs?* This is what I will call the *fundamental question* that must be addressed in any attempt to evaluate the justice or injustice of our nation's drug policy. The fundamental question asks for a *rationale* for our policy. The search for a rationale involves an attempt to find moral reasons that will *justify* our policy of punishing drug users. The point of this book is to attempt to answer this fundamental question. I will defend the conclusion that drug use should *not* be criminalized and that drug users should *not* be punished.

I suspect that people often fail to reach the conclusion I will defend because they begin by asking the *wrong* question. They start their examination of drug policy by addressing a different issue. This seems odd and surprising. The fundamental question

I have asked seems straightforward and appropriate – even if it proves difficult to answer. Why would anyone purport to evaluate our drug policy by addressing some *other* question? In the United States today, a national debate about our country's drug policy is under way. Still, I fear that most public debates about our drug policy are less productive than they might be. Fair-minded and unbiased observers fail to reach the right conclusion because they begin by asking the wrong question. Too often, debates about existing drug policy address the topic, *Should drug use be decriminalized?* A different version of this same question is, *Should we stop punishing drug users?* I will try to show why this latter question is not the most fundamental question to ask in evaluating our drug policy.

The question I believe should be asked – Should drug use be criminalized? – and the question that is generally asked – Should drug use be decriminalized? – are different, and the difference is important. The right question demands a justification for our existing policy. It asks whether we have a good reason for doing what we now do to drug users. The wrong question does not demand a justification for our existing policy. It asks whether we have a good reason *not* to do what we now do to drug users. In a debate about existing policy, those who support the status quo gain an enormous advantage by beginning with the second question rather than with the first. This advantage is wholly unwarranted. When debates focus on the issue of whether drug use should be *de*criminalized, critics of our policy are forced to identify the benefits of changing it. When they try to describe these benefits, their adversaries can raise doubts about whether these benefits will indeed materialize if our laws are altered. It is very hard to predict exactly how our society would change if we stopped punishing drug users. No one should have much confidence in the accuracy of his or her predictions; too many unknown variables will affect the nature of a society in which drug use is no longer criminalized. The debate is likely to end in a cloud of uncertainty. Critics of our existing policy will not have been persuasive in demonstrating the advantages of change. In the minds of many fair-minded and impartial observers, defenders of the status quo will have triumphed. At the very least, the debate will end in a stalemate. No clear conclusions will have been reached.

Notice what is missing from the kind of debate I have described. First, this debate is almost certain to lose sight of principles of *justice* – the most important consideration to keep in mind when evaluating our criminal laws. A debate about the advantages or disadvantages of *change* is likely to become focused on whether existing policy *works* better than some alternative to it. Almost inevitably, the debate will center on how we can best attain the goals toward which we believe our policy should aim. Justice will probably seem unimportant if we are fixated on objectives. Justice should not be conceptualized as a *goal* our policies should try to achieve, but as a *constraint* that limits what we are allowed to do in pursuing our objectives. In other words, justice rules out some strategies that we otherwise would be permitted to adopt in trying to attain our ends. As we will see, even the most outspoken critics of our drug policy tend to neglect these constraints.[1] For justice to regain its central place, we must begin by asking the right question.

Something else is missing from a debate that begins by asking the wrong question. In a debate that asks whether drug use should be *de*criminalized, those who support our existing policy need not utter a single word in its defense. Their job is too easy. They can simply sit back and wait for their opponents to make predictions about the advantages of decriminalization and then challenge the accuracy of those predictions. Why do they win the debate when they have said absolutely nothing on behalf of the position they endorse? We should not punish people simply because we are unable to demonstrate the benefits of *not* punishing them. Any policy that resorts to punishment requires a justification. We should not assume that what we are doing is right unless someone can prove that it is wrong. We must always be prepared

---

1 Philosophical input on drug policy has been almost nonexistent. Exceptions include Douglas Husak, *Drugs and Rights* (Cambridge: Cambridge University Press, 1992); Steven Luper-Foy and Curtis Brown, eds., *Drugs, Morality, and the Law* (New York: Garland, 1994); and Douglas Husak, *Legalize This!* (London: Verso, 2002).

to show why what we are doing is right. If neither side provides good reasons, or if both sides provide reasons that are equally persuasive, victory in the debate should not be awarded to the side that supports the status quo – when the status quo involves criminalization. Punishment is the most terrible thing that a state can do to its citizens; it is the most powerful weapon in the government's arsenal. The criminal sanction should not be invoked casually; it always requires a compelling defense. Those who favor punishments for drug users must explain why they think this policy is fair and just. No one should be deprived of liberty unless there are excellent reasons to do so. The fundamental question, then, is not whether we have good reasons *not* to punish drug users – so that drug use should be decriminalized – but whether we have good reasons to (continue to) punish people who use drugs.

My point is not simply that the burden of proof on this issue has been placed on the wrong side – although that is certainly true. Nor is my point that we should not allow one side in the debate to gain an unfair rhetorical advantage over the other – although that is certainly true as well. My point is that the debate cannot proceed sensibly unless it begins with a reason in favor of punishing people who use drugs. How can we possibly decide whether we should change our policy unless we know why we have that policy in the first place? Unless a reason to punish drug users has been put on the table, opponents of the status quo have nothing to which they can respond. In other words, an effective argument for decriminalization must rebut an argument for criminalization. Without an argument for criminalization, there is nothing to rebut.

Imagine the progress – or lack of progress – in a debate about *any* policy if its opponents were forced to describe the advantages of change, while its supporters were not made to defend the status quo. Imagine a debate about the institution of slavery prior to the Civil War. Suppose that abolitionists were required to make detailed predictions about how society would benefit if slaves were freed. Even the most eloquent critic of slavery could not have had much confidence in her forecasts. The inevitable controversy about the accuracy of these predictions would distract us from the most basic objection to slavery – its injustice. No one should conclude that the institution of slavery should be preserved because its defenders are able to raise doubts about what might happen if the abolitionist alternative were implemented. At some point, defenders of slavery should be forced to defend slavery. Once a defense of slavery is on the table, abolitionists have something to which they can respond.

What is true of slavery is true of any institution or social policy (such as our drug policy) that resorts to punishment. At some point, defenders of drug prohibition must defend drug prohibition. If our criminal laws are to be *just*, each criminal law must be *justified*. To justify a particular criminal law is to provide compelling reasons to punish people who break that law. We need reasons that are powerful because punishment is the worst thing our state can do to us. Punishment infringes rights and liberties that we usually take for granted. The justification must become more persuasive as punishments become increasingly severe – involving jail or prison, rather than a small monetary fine. We need very good reasons before we put people behind bars, and defenders of our drug policy must be pressed to tell us what these reasons are.

Sometimes we fail to demand a justification for our criminal laws because we mistakenly suppose that imprisonment is not really a major hardship. In the United States today, we resort to severe punishments so routinely that we forget how devastating incarceration really is. We hear that criminals sentenced to a "mere" six months in prison are given a "slap on the wrist." Or we read that criminals are confined in "country-club" prisons. No one who has ever been jailed or imprisoned is likely to share these remarkable attitudes. Prisoners lose their liberty and most of their rights. They are deprived of their family, friends, job, and community. Their days are passed in unproductive idleness. Prison life is degrading, demoralizing, and dangerous. Once released, offenders are less employable and often forfeit their rights to vote or to receive public benefits and services. Punishment has a negative impact on the lives of their spouse and children. These effects should not be imposed lightly. To ensure that our society is just, we must insist on a very convincing rationale before we resort to punishment.

Everyone with a serious interest in our drug policy should be urged to begin the debate by wrestling with the fundamental question I have posed. Ask yourself – and ask your friends and neighbors – Do you really believe that people should be punished for using drugs? Do you think that the laws that put people in jail simply for using drugs are justified? If so, why? Why does justice allow us to punish drug users? Do not suppose that you must describe the advantages of decriminalization until an argument for criminalization has been given first. If the question I have raised cannot be answered to your satisfaction, you should conclude that people who use drugs should *not* be punished – for no one should be punished in the absence of a very good reason.

What counts as a good enough reason to inflict punishment? There is no simple formula; reasonable minds will be persuaded by different arguments. Despite inevitable disagreement, we should notice how easy it is to answer the fundamental question I have asked if we use almost any other crime – that is, almost any crime other than the crime of drug use – as an example. We send robbers, rapists, and murderers to jail. Suppose that someone asks (rhetorically) whether people who commit these acts should (continue to) be punished. She challenges legislators to justify their decisions to enact these statutes – to provide a good reason to punish robbers, rapists, or murderers. Her challenge is easily met. These people *deserve* to be punished because they have violated the rights of their victims and harmed them severely. We all have rights not to be robbed, raped, or murdered. Anyone who violates these rights deserves to be punished.

Because it is so easy to justify punishment when virtually any other crimes are used as examples, there is no real controversy about whether these offenses should be repealed. No sensible person opposes the punishment of murderers, rapists, or robbers. But the straightforward answer I have given in the cases of robbery, rape, or murder is unavailable in the case of drug use. If there is a good reason to punish drug users, it cannot be the same reason we can give if we are challenged to explain why robbers, rapists, and murderers should be punished. Each of these criminals has harmed and violated the rights of their victims. Thus they *deserve* to be punished.

It is crucial to recognize that my answer to the rhetorical question of why murderers and rapists should be punished does not depend on conjecture. It hazards no predictions about how rates of murder or rape would differ if these acts were legalized. Thus my rationale for punishment differs from that of Peter de Marneffe, author of the opposing view in this book. He claims, "It is an axiom of enlightened public policy that no criminal penalty is justified unless it deters conduct that is harmful or unfair in some way. The justification for any criminal law thus presupposes that it has some deterrent effect. This is no less true of laws prohibiting murder than it is of laws prohibiting the manufacture and sale of drugs."[2] Unlike de Marneffe, I do not believe that the rationale for criminalizing murder and rape depends on empirical speculation about whether these acts are deterred by punishment. Instead, persons who perpetrate these acts *deserve* to be punished. The state is never justified in punishing someone unless he or she deserves it. I regard this claim as an elementary principle of justice.

Of course, philosophers since the time of Plato are accustomed to disagreement in their attempts to identify and defend principles of justice. Anyone who proposes that justice allows or precludes affirmative action in university admissions, for example, should be prepared for massive controversy. The principle of justice I invoke here is not comparable. My principle is so obvious that I find it hard it believe that anyone disagrees with it. We can anticipate lots of disagreement about how this principle *applies* to the topic of drug decriminalization. But this disagreement is not about the *content* of the principle itself. I assume that all parties to the debate concur in my claim that a compelling reason is needed to justify the infliction of punishment, and any acceptable

2 De Marneffe, this volume, p. 191.

reason must explain why the person to be punished deserves punishment.

Despite my confidence that virtually no one disagrees with my principle of justice or my formulation of the fundamental question that must be addressed in evaluating our drug policy, I must admit that my approach *has* encountered some resistance – even from knowledgeable reformers who are unhappy with the status quo. In a recent and comprehensive book, Robert MacCoun and Peter Reuter – two academics whose expertise in drug policy cannot be questioned – discuss the standards by which alternative approaches to drug policy should be evaluated. Among the standards they reject is what they call the "philosophical standard." They write:

> If a society were starting from scratch, the burden might well be placed on those who would prohibit drug use. . . . If this standard were applied today, the current laws would be changed unless prohibiters could make a convincing case for the current laws. Though some reformers write as if this were the applicable standard, they are mostly talking to themselves, since it is [*sic*] seems unlikely that the American public is ready to accept this standard.[3]

Since I endorse the "philosophical standard," I believe that MacCoun and Reuter's reasons for rejecting it merit a reply. First, I fail to see why these authors believe that the principles of justice that should be used to evaluate our drug policy should differ depending on whether or not we are starting our society "from scratch." In fact, virtually no real societies are ever begun from scratch. We can certainly imagine sailors shipwrecked on a desert island or astronauts colonizing the Moon who might be said to create an entirely new social order. For the most part, however, these scenarios are the stuff of fiction. In the real world, we must evaluate the policy options for the societies we already have. Why should those who support these policies be spared the need to defend them? MacCoun and Reuter seemingly suppose that

3 See Robert J. MacCoun and Peter Reuter, *Drug War Heresies* (Cambridge: Cambridge University Press, 2001), p. 324, n. 1.

the status quo needs no defense. But this cannot be correct – especially when the status quo involves punishment. Today, tomorrow, next week, and next month, Americans will be punished simply for using a drug for recreational purposes. What justifies this policy? We should not answer, with MacCoun and Reuter, that those who ask such questions are talking "only to themselves." Instead, those who ask such questions are talking to *each* of us – to each of us who cares about whether or not our social polices are just.

In the final sentence of the preceding quotation, MacCoun and Reuter suggest that the fundamental question I have posed is the wrong question to ask in evaluating our drug policy because "it seems unlikely that the American public is ready to accept [it]." I am skeptical that MacCoun and Reuter are correct about what "the American public" is ready to accept. I find it hard to believe that the American public really believes that justice allows our state to subject us to punishment without telling us why. But this is not my main worry with MacCoun and Reuter's reason for rejecting (what they call) the philosophical standard. In deciding what criteria to apply in evaluating competing ideas about drug policy, the test is not what the public *does* accept, but what the public *should* accept. In other words, the test is moral. The basic moral claim I make in this book is that no one should be punished in the absence of powerful reasons that explain why the punishment is deserved. I would not be persuaded to retract my basic claim because I was assured that the public did not accept it. Instead, I would redouble my efforts to convince those who disagree with me. If all proposals about how to reform our drug policy could be resolved by determining whether members of the public already accept them, there would be no point in trying to persuade them to change their mind.

Analogies are helpful in allowing us to appreciate what is mistaken about MacCoun and Reuter's approach. I trust that these authors would not be so dismissive of "philosophical standards" if the justice or injustice of other social policies were assessed. Return to my example of the institution of slavery prior to our Civil War. Would these authors suppose that justice is somehow more tolerant of slavery in a society that condones it than in a society that does not? Do they believe that those who supported slavery had the burden of explaining why they thought it to be just only in a society begun "from scratch"? Would they be persuaded to abandon their judgment that slavery is unjust if they could be convinced that the public did not accept their views? I am confident that any reasonable person – including MacCoun and Reuter – would answer these questions in the negative.

The principle of justice I cite – that a compelling reason is needed to justify the infliction of punishment, and any acceptable reason must explain why the person punished deserves to be punished – is extremely important, even if it is elementary. One way to evaluate proposed rationales for drug criminalization is to determine whether they can be expressed in terms of desert. Even without providing a philosophically deep or sophisticated theory of desert, it is easy to appreciate that some possible rationales for drug criminalization fail this test. Let me illustrate how many (otherwise plausible) rationales for punishing drug users can be shown to be deficient, once we recognize that they cannot be expressed in terms of desert.

My first example is what is called *harm-reduction*. Many sensible and enlightened commentators propose that the best drug policy is whatever will minimize harm.[4] Their basic insight is that current drug policy initiatives are almost always evaluated by a criterion we should reject: the test of *use-reduction* (or *prevalence-reduction*). In other words, at the present time, no suggestion about how to improve our policy will be accepted unless it offers the potential to reduce the numbers of persons who use drugs. Theorists who favor a standard of harm-reduction point out that the total amount of harm that drugs cause in our society might actually decrease, even though the number of drug users would increase. If the average harm caused per user were reduced, total social harm might go down while the number of users went up.

---

4 Many influential books have defended harm-reduction perspectives. See, for example, James A. Inciardi and Lana D. Harrison, eds., *Harm Reduction: National and International Perspectives* (London: Sage, 2000).

The most promising harm-reduction initiatives are needle exchange programs for heroin addicts and medical programs for
patients whose symptoms are alleviated by smoking marijuana.
Both of these ideas can effectively reduce harm in society. Every
scientific study has concluded that needle exchange programs
can reduce the spread of acquired immunodeficiency syndrome
(AIDS) among heroin addicts without increasing the number of
users. And it seems cruel to deny effective medicine to patients
with diseases such as glaucoma whose symptoms are relieved
by smoking marijuana. Only a standard fixated on use-reduction
would reject these initiatives.

I readily admit that our drug policy would be improved expo-
nentially were we to replace our use-reduction criterion of success
with a harm-reduction model. Any reasonable person should be
receptive to ideas that decrease overall harm. Still, I think we
would be hasty to conclude that all of our social policies should
be evaluated by a harm-reduction test. The social policies that
should be least amenable to a harm-reduction standard are those
that involve punishments. Our criminal justice system is, above
all, a system of justice. The just society is not necessarily the society that minimizes total harm. As I have indicated, justice is
a constraint that occasionally prevents the state from adopting
initiatives that cause less harm overall. The presumption of in-
nocence, the requirement of proof beyond a reasonable doubt,
and similar protections we afford to criminal defendants are hard
to defend on harm-reduction grounds. These principles, I submit,
are derived from considerations of justice. If and when justice and
harm-reduction proposals conflict in the arena of criminal justice,
I believe that the former, rather than the latter, should guide our
decisions.

To be sure, some of the commentators who endorse a harm-
reduction approach to drug policy also believe that drug users
should be punished. They allege that, in general, the best way to
reduce harm is to reduce use, and the most effective way to reduce
use is to punish users. These claims are controversial and probably
false, but let us assume for the sake of argument that they are
true. Even so, these allegations cannot provide the rationale for
criminalization we seek; they do not answer our fundamental

question by justifying the punishments of drug users. The reason is simple. No one deserves to be punished simply because less harm would be produced in society if he were punished than if he were not. The (assumed) fact that less harm would be caused by punishing someone does not thereby *justify* the punishment or show that it is *deserved*.

Peter de Marneffe's efforts provide my second example of a possible answer to our fundamental question that should be rejected because it cannot be expressed in terms of desert. His sophisticated and balanced argument against drug legalization is unabashedly paternalistic. De Marneffe focuses on the use of heroin, perhaps unique among recreational activities because it is intensely pleasurable. Since its pleasures are so overwhelming, many people – including adolescents – need lots of help in resisting them. Some of those users who succumb to the allure of heroin suffer gravely as a result, losing precious opportunities they may never regain. De Marneffe admits that many users of heroin will not suffer this fate. Some people (let us suppose they are named Smith) will be able to enjoy the pleasures of heroin without losing valuable opportunities. But their reasons for wanting to use heroin are outweighed by the reasons of other persons (call them Jones) who want it to be banned. Thus, heroin should be prohibited.

To evaluate de Marneffe's argument, we must remember what is at stake. If his rationale is not designed to answer our fundamental question, we may put it aside. Suppose, however, that it is designed to provide a justification for criminalization. Suppose, that is, that it is intended to justify *punishing* drug users (and users of heroin in particular). Does it succeed? Let us see how de Marneffe's rationale fares when expressed in terms of desert. His original claim is that some persons – call them Smith – should be *prohibited* from using heroin because other persons – named Jones – would be unable to resist it if it were legalized, and that Jones's use of heroin would be bad for him because it would reduce his opportunities. When understood as a rationale for criminalization, however, his claim should be rephrased, and the difference is crucial. The new claim is that Smith should be *punished* for using heroin because Jones would be unable to resist it if it were legalized, and Jones's use of heroin would be bad for him. I submit that the latter claim looks much less persuasive than the former. To confirm the implausibility of the newly phrased rationale, simply apply the test I described earlier – the test of expressing the rationale in terms of desert. Can it really be true that Smith *deserves* to be punished for doing something because if he were *not* punished for doing it, Jones would succumb to the temptation to do it too, and Jones could not do it without losing opportunities? How does this rationale establish that Smith deserves to be punished for what he has done? I cannot *prove* that this rationale fails to meet the high standards we should require before concluding that Smith's punishment is justified. Again, there is no formula to decide whether a rationale for criminalization should be accepted. But I do not agree that the foregoing argument succeeds in showing why the punishments of heroin users are deserved.

In no other context do we believe that the Smiths of the world deserve to be punished, despite the fact that they are harming neither themselves nor others, because the Joneses of the world would be unable to mimic their behavior without jeopardizing their future. Consider other dangerous activities. When Edmund Hillary succeeded in scaling Mount Everest, he unwittingly created a cottage industry in which unskilled climbers by the thousands attempted to duplicate his feat. Hundreds have died – a fate worse than the mere loss of opportunities. What should we think about Hillary's influence? We might differ about whether he merits our praise and admiration. But no one would conclude that Hillary deserved to be *punished* for his deed. Why is heroin use so different? As far as I can tell, de Marneffe's only basis for distinguishing my example of mountain climbing from that of heroin use is that the latter is so much more pleasurable than the former. Whether this alleged difference suffices to justify *punishing* users of heroin is dubious at best.

If de Marneffe's empirical assumptions about heroin are correct, many strategies should be employed to dissuade people from using heroin. Education and taxation are foremost among these devices. Admittedly, they work imperfectly; some people will use heroin if these strategies are implemented. But more than a million people used heroin regularly in 2004, even though heroin users are subject to punishment. I fail to see how the paternalistic rationale de Marneffe constructs shows that users of heroin deserve to be punished. Although it is hard to be precise about when a rationale is good enough to justify criminalization and punishment, I conclude that the foregoing two attempts fail.

My case for decriminalization is that the arguments for criminalization are not sufficiently persuasive to justify the infliction of punishment. In other words, the best reason to *de*criminalize drug use is that the reasons to *criminalize* drug use are not good enough. This simple explanation in favor of decriminalization is that those who support criminalization have not made their case. I admit that this argument for decriminalization seems unexciting. It lacks the rhetorical appeal of calls to eliminate "taxation without representation" or to secure "one man, one vote." No lofty principle such as freedom of speech or freedom of religion is at stake. But perhaps I needlessly denigrate my own argument for decriminalization. The principle of justice I invoke – that no one should be punished unless there are compelling reasons to do so that are grounded in the desert of the offender – may be the most fundamental principle in a free society committed to justice for all.

This principle should be applied not only to our drug policy. *Each* criminal law must be justified. Where will we find these rationales? The burden to produce justifications for our criminal laws is placed squarely on *us* – the citizens of a democratic state. Our failure to require a justification for our criminal laws has contributed to the phenomenon of *overcriminalization*. We have far too many criminal laws in the United States – perhaps as many as 300,000. The stigma associated with a criminal conviction has been diluted almost to the vanishing point, since many new offenses punish behavior that is more laughable than reprehensible. For example, federal law imposes criminal penalties on persons who sell mixtures of two kinds of turpentine, walk dogs on the grounds of federal buildings, or disturb mud in a cave in a national park. It is much easier to pass than to repeal a criminal law, so the number of crimes grows steadily each year. Greater numbers of crimes help to produce more and more criminals, many of whom fill our jails or prisons. More than 2 million people are presently incarcerated in the United States. This statistic is a national embarrassment. Why are we so quick to resort to severe punishments? At what point will we decide that too many of our citizens are behind bars? If we are serious about reducing the size of the prison population and reversing the trend toward overcriminalization, there is no better place to begin than by scrutinizing the rationale for punishing drug users.

According to the FBI's annual uniform crime report, more than 1.5 million people were arrested on drug charges in 2002, roughly 80 percent of them for simple possession. Marijuana users made up nearly half of this total, with some 693,000 arrests that year, 88 percent of them for simple possession. The marijuana arrest figure is down slightly from the all-time high of 734,000 arrests achieved during the final year of the Clinton administration. By contrast, in 1993, the number of arrests was 380,000. More than 6 million Americans have been arrested on marijuana charges in the past decade alone. Drug arrests made up about 10 percent of all arrests and constitute the single largest category of arrests. Drug arrests are more than twice as frequent as arrests for all violent crimes combined (620,000). Marijuana possession accounted for almost 40 percent of drug arrests, followed by heroin and cocaine possession (21 percent), and "other dangerous non-narcotic drugs" (16 percent). Simple possession constituted four-fifths of all drug arrests in 2001.[5]

What *is* the rationale for these punitive policies? Since the state does not tell us, we have no choice but to guess. Again, it is hard to advance a defense of drug decriminalization until those who support the status quo produce a rationale in favor of criminalization. In the absence of a defense, my nearly impossible task is to prove a negative – that no good reasons to punish drug users exist.

5 Perhaps the best source for data on illicit drugs and criminal justice is the Bureau of Justice Statistics, *Sourcebook of Criminal Justice Statistics* online (http://www.albany.edu/sourcebook).

All I can hope to accomplish is to respond to the most common arguments offered on behalf of criminalization. In Chapter 3, I will evaluate four such arguments: criminalization is justified in order to protect public health, to protect our children, to reduce crime, or to preserve morality. I will conclude that none of these rationales should persuade us that punishment is deserved simply for the act of using drugs.

3   Reasons to Criminalize Drug Use

E ACH of the four rationales I will examine is designed to answer what I have called the fundamental question about
our drug policy: Should recreational users of (some) drugs be
punished? Should drug use be criminalized? Where should we
look for possible answers to these questions – for alleged justifications of criminalization? Since there is no "official" rationale
for our drug policy, the most sensible way to proceed is to examine those arguments that have actually been given by the most
knowledgeable and thoughtful individuals who have spoken on
its behalf. The most well-known defenders of our policy include
William Bennett, the country's first and most influential "drug
czar," and James Q. Wilson, former chairman of the National
Advisory Council for Drug Abuse Prevention and one of the most
distinguished and widely respected criminologists in America today. In addition, I will make frequent reference to the publica-
tions of the Office of National Drug Control Policy (ONDCP) – the
government office charged with establishing policies, priorities,
and objectives for drug policy in the United States. Although the
ONDCP has no authority to make law, it is perhaps the best source
of an authoritative defense of the law.

Drugs and Health

Protecting our physical and mental health is one of the most important functions of the state. Might this objective justify the
punishment of persons who use (some) drugs for recreational

purposes? Does the need to protect our health and well-being provide the rationale for criminalization?

It is telling that few prohibitionists endorse this rationale explicitly. No one seems willing to say, "The state is justified in punishing drug users because illicit drugs are bad for their health." Clearly, however, this rationale is adopted implicitly. Anyone who proposes to decriminalize a given drug is certain to be informed of an empirical study that allegedly shows the drug to pose risks to the health of those who use it. A plea to decriminalize the use of ecstasy, for example, is bound to lead prohibitionists to counter that ecstasy is unsafe. Similar findings are cited whenever reformers suggest that marijuana should be legalized. These allegations may provide a perfectly sensible answer to the question "Should I use ecstasy or marijuana?" But how are they responsive to my fundamental question about criminalization? These allegations would be irrelevant unless those who support the status quo believe that the goal of protecting health provides a good reason to *punish* drug users.

How should we begin to evaluate this possible rationale for drug prohibition? Two points are fairly clear. First, we should concede that drugs *are* often bad for the health of those who use them. More precisely, illicit drugs pose *risks* to physical and psychological well-being. Of course, these risks vary in degree from one drug to another. Moreover, the extent of these risks is controversial – a matter to which I will return. Still, anyone who wants to minimize health risks is advised not to use drugs for recreational purposes.

The second clear point is that this objective provides an exceptionally strange rationale for drug prohibition. Although the state has a central role in protecting the health of its citizens, it does not ordinarily perform this function by punishing the very persons whose health it endeavors to protect. The Food and Drug Administration, for example, provides a valuable service by ensuring that consumers do not get sick by eating spoiled meat. Criminal penalties can be imposed on sellers of adulterated foods. But no one has ever proposed to put people in jail for eating foods they know to be unhealthy. The idea that people should be punished for taking risks to their health is extraordinary – and very hard to accept in a state that limits the scope of the criminal law.

Prohibitionists themselves must recognize this rationale to be implausible, since they tend to endorse it with reservations. When challenged about whether this objective *really* provides the justification for criminalization, they often emphasize not only the importance of protecting the health of the individual, but also the public expense incurred when people make unhealthy choices. Risky behavior raises insurance premiums for everyone and places a financial burden on health services provided by the state at taxpayer expense. The fact that the cost to the taxpaying public is mentioned so frequently shows how uncomfortable prohibitionists are with the principle that people should be thrown into jail in order to protect their health. In any event, this new emphasis does little to improve the plausibility of the rationale. The principle that people should be punished in order to reduce insurance premiums and conserve public resources is not much more credible than the original rationale it is designed to supplement or replace. This principle proves far too much. If applied consistently, it would authorize the criminalization of *any* activity – such as overeating or playing extreme sports – that burdened state health resources.

Beyond these two clear points, the issue becomes murky. We might clarify the matter by inquiring *how* criminalization could possibly succeed in improving health. Two accounts might be defended. First, punishment might deter current drug users from persisting in their unhealthy behavior. Drug users might be "scared straight" by the shock of punishment, thereby avoiding further damage to their health and well-being. Second, the threat of punishment might deter those who do not use drugs from beginning. Prospective users who never start will not risk the physical and psychological hazards of drug use.

It is unlikely that criminalization will improve health and well-being in either of these two ways. Consider the first. It supposes that the health of drug users will improve (or not deteriorate further) if they are sent to prison. One difficulty with this account is that it assumes that prisoners will stop using drugs. Surveys in 2004 indicated, however, that about 10 percent of all prisoners use illicit drugs while incarcerated.[1] The real difficulty with this account, however, is more fundamental. Prison is obviously deleterious to health – far more deleterious than drugs. We could easily *imagine* a drug that is so detrimental to health that nearly anything that could be done to prevent people from continuing to use it would promote their safety in the long run. Someone might be better off in jail than free to take a drug that killed significant numbers of those who persist in using it. Fortunately, no existing recreational drug is nearly so destructive – with the possible exception of tobacco.

Arguably, the state interest in deterring people from behavior that poses substantial risks to their health and well-being might be sufficiently strong to justify the infliction of criminal penalties – but only when the risks are great and punishments are not severe. Consider, for example, laws requiring drivers of cars to wear seat belts. Of course, these laws are controversial and unpopular. Yet they are far easier to justify than laws prohibiting the use of recreational drugs (when these laws are construed to protect our health). The penalty for violating seat-belt laws is minimal; usually, only a small fine is imposed. Since sanctions are so trivial, a case might be made that these laws really do serve the interest of those they punish. Enforcement increases (by a small amount) the likelihood that drivers will buckle their seat belts and survive a crash. Payment of a fine is a minor hardship if it succeeds in decreasing a substantial risk to safety. But it is hard to argue that laws prohibiting the use of recreational drugs are actually in the interest of the very people they punish. At the present time, the penalties imposed on offenders are far too severe to make this claim plausible. As sanctions increase in severity, the "cure" of punishment becomes worse than the "disease" – the risk to well-being that the law is designed to prevent.

---

1 See David Wyatt Seal, et al., "A Qualitative Study of Substance Use and Sexual Behavior among 18- to 29-Year-Old Men While Incarcerated in the United States," 31 *Health Education & Behavior* (2004), p. 775.

The second account of how prohibition might succeed in protecting public health is somewhat more credible. Health will be enhanced if the threat of punishment deters people who do not use drugs from beginning to do so. This account, of course, depends on three assumptions. First, health will not be protected unless criminalization is a reasonably effective deterrent. If the threat of punishment does not dissuade people from experimenting with drugs, no health gains will be achieved. Since about 15 million Americans use illicit drugs each month, the deterrent efficacy of prohibition would appear to be weak.[2] Second, the health of those who *are* deterred from experimentation will be preserved only if they do not substitute more or equally dangerous drugs for those they forgo. We should not assume that those who would use illicit drugs but for the threat of criminal penalties will choose to eat vegetables and fruit rather than to consume some other unhealthy (but licit) substance.

I want to focus on yet a third assumption that is obviously crucial to any account of how health might be improved by the prohibition of recreational drug use. We cannot fully assess the plausibility of this rationale unless we understand *how* risky drugs really are. If these risks are small, we would hardly be justified in waging a warlike effort in order to prevent them. But if these risks are substantial, we are on firmer ground when we take drastic steps to deter drug use. We tolerate seat-belt laws not only because fines are modest, but also because they have been proved to reduce a risk that actually kills some 40,000 motorists each year. Seat belts have also been shown to be effective in reducing the severity of hundreds of thousands of nonfatal injuries. What are the comparable figures for drug use? Before we are led to punish drug users to protect their health, we should demand convincing evidence that the drugs we prohibit are unhealthy. Where is this evidence? We should not be persuaded by anecdotes – stories of people who swear that their health has been ruined by

---

2 See Jeffrey Fagan, "Do Criminal Sanctions Deter Drug Offenders?" in Doris MacKenzie and Craig Uchida, eds., *Drugs and Crime: Evaluating Public Policy Initiatives* (Thousand Oaks, CA: Sage, 1994).

drugs. We could match these anecdotes with colorful accounts of aged individuals who attribute their longevity to their daily consumption of tobacco. Nor should we be persuaded by studies that indicate that users of a given drug "might" encounter "some" risk. We must ask, How great a risk, and what is the probability of its occurrence? A complete response to this possible rationale for selective prohibition must try to assess the extent of health risks caused by the use of illicit drugs.

Epidemiological studies are the easiest and most obvious way to identify the hazards of any substance – tobacco, for example. If tobacco causes cancer, one would expect that the cancer rates of smokers would be substantially higher than those of nonsmokers. Someone who maintained that tobacco causes cancer would be embarrassed if data showed that smokers and nonsmokers were equally likely to have cancer. Of course, these studies confirm our worst fears about tobacco. What do epidemiological studies tend to show about the effects of illicit drugs?[3]

If we divide the population into two groups – those who have used illicit drugs and those who have not – no existing data show the former to be less healthy than the latter. From a health perspective, the 80 or 90 million Americans above the age of 12 who have used illicit drugs are not readily distinguishable from the somewhat greater number of Americans who have abstained throughout their lifetime. But two important qualifications are needed. First, existing studies are less helpful in revealing *long-term* risks to health. Few in the United States used illicit drugs prior to the mid-1960s. The incidence of illicit drug use peaked about 1979, when about 14 percent of the population took drugs on a weekly basis. Most of those who consumed the greatest amounts of drugs in those years are between the ages of 40 and 50 at the beginning of the 21st century. Although the consequences of drug use to their physical health and psychological well-being are not apparent today, the negative effects may become manifest as these users age. But this conjecture provides no reason

---

3 For a nice survey, see Denise B. Kandel, "The Social Demography of Drug Use," 69 *The Milbank Quarterly* 365 (1991).

to criminalize drug use in the present. We should be extremely reluctant to punish people to protect them from health hazards we *know* to exist. If these risks are merely speculative, the case for punishment evaporates. We might as well speculate that the use of illicit drugs actually improves our health. After all, nearly all researchers now admit that moderate amounts of alcohol correlate with reduced risks of coronary heart disease. We know better than simply to assume without evidence that recreational drug use *must* be very bad for our health in the long run.

The second qualification is more worrisome. Suppose we divide the population of illicit drug users further – into moderate and heavy users. A minority of users have consumed massive amounts of drugs over extended periods. Our evidence about the health effects of heavy, long-term illicit drug use – supplemented by data from other countries, where illicit drug use was prevalent at an earlier time than in the United States – does not uniformly show great cause for alarm. Suppose, however, that the latter group turns out to be substantially less healthy than the former. Imagine, in other words, that the health hazards of illicit drug use resembled those of alcohol, whose heavy users suffer most of the harm. In this event, the controversy would shift to a different issue – a normative issue about criminalization, rather than an empirical issue about the effects of drugs. How would this finding provide a rationale for punishing *all* users of illicit drugs – even those whose drug use does *not* jeopardize their health? After all, moderate users greatly outnumber persons who are heavy users over extended periods. Moreover, heavy users tend to be unlike moderate users; they are far more likely to be poor. What is the justification for punishing everyone who uses an illicit drug in order to protect a small minority from possibly becoming less healthy?

Even apart from this difficulty, how can we hope to assess the risks of drug use and decide whether they are acceptable? *Aggregate* statistics are helpful in answering this question. According to estimates of the ONCDP, about 25,000 Americans die each year as a result of using illicit drugs. This statistic is not very informative unless it is placed alongside data about the number of fatalities caused by other activities. Here, as elsewhere, aggregate statistics about *licit* drugs provide the most obvious basis of comparison. First, consider the facts about licit drugs used for medical purposes. Approximately 100,000 people die each year as a result of adverse reactions to medications, making prescription drugs one of the leading causes of death in the country.[4] These deaths are not due to mistakes by doctors who prescribe drugs or by patients who take them. Fatal drug reactions occur because virtually all medications have bad side effects in many people, even when taken in proper doses. The assumption that illicit drugs are unsafe, and prescription drugs are safe, is perhaps the greatest myth surrounding the debate about criminalization.

Aggregate statistics about licit drugs used for recreational purposes are an even more obvious basis of comparison. Each year, tobacco kills at least 430,000 people in the United States. The number of annual fatalities caused by alcohol is more controversial, but nearly all estimates exceed 100,000. By contrast, illicit drugs seem benign. For example, no one has ever been known to die as a result of smoking marijuana. Consider the 25,000 casualties said to be caused by other illicit drugs. A minority of these deaths are actually caused by drugs; a majority result from diseases such as AIDS and hepatitis that are spread by sharing contaminated needles. About 2,500 are caused intentionally; 1,600 more are due to injuries inflicted "accidentally or purposely." Illicit drugs themselves cause remarkably few fatalities.

Of course, these aggregate figures do not give us much insight unless they take into account the fact that many more people use licit than illicit drugs. Naturally, we would expect to see more health problems caused by whatever drugs happen to be the most popular. Nonetheless, once we adjust our statistics to reflect this fact – and describe the risk of various drugs by the ratio of fatalities per user – we reach the very same conclusion. When the risk of a given drug is represented by the percentage of users who are killed by it, nicotine is still the most lethal drug by a wide margin.

4 See J. S. Cohen, *Overdose: The Case against the Drug Companies* (New York: Jeremy P. Tarcher/Putnam, 2001).

About one-quarter of all persons who smoke a pack of cigarettes daily lose ten to fifteen years of their life. Illicit drugs are far less hazardous. If criminalization is designed to prevent users from risking their life, our society has criminalized the wrong drugs.

The point is not simply one of consistency. The question is not "If the state endeavors to protect public health by punishing people who use cocaine, why does not the state also punish people who smoke tobacco and drink alcohol?" After all, problems of consistency can be solved in either of two ways – either by repealing laws against illicit drug use or by enacting laws against the consumption of alcohol and tobacco. The point is that the latter alternative is unthinkable. No one explicitly recommends that we should throw smokers and drinkers into jail in order to reduce the health problems caused by these licit drugs. Why not? The best answer is that punishing smokers or drinkers would be unjust. The point is that the criminalization of illicit drugs is unjust for the very same reason that applies to proposals to criminalize the use of licit drugs.

So far, my statistics about the relative risks of licit and illicit drugs involve only fatalities. But the health problems caused by drugs include not only death, but also various diseases and illnesses that lower the quality of life. Allegations about the health hazards of illicit drugs are many and varied; it is impossible even to scratch the surface. Drug use has been said to kill brain cells, impair memory and cognition, undermine motivation and performance, produce psychosis and insanity, destroy the immune system, hamper sex drive and reproduction, and generally contribute to hospital emergencies. Obviously, all of these allegations must be assessed drug by drug. How can we begin to get a handle on the health hazards of illicit drugs?

Again, licit drugs provide an obvious basis of comparison. Illicit drugs tend to be less injurious than many licit drugs, recreational or medical. Legal medications cause between 1 million and 5.5 million hospitalizations every year. Approximately 70,000 of these annual hospitalizations are caused by common anti-inflammatories such as Advil and Tylenol. But licit drugs used for recreational purposes provide an even more appropriate basis of comparison. In 2003, 28 percent of admissions to intensive care units were related to drug problems; 14 percent involved tobacco, 9 percent involved alcohol, and 5 percent involved other drugs. Tobacco is a major cause of coronary artery disease, peripheral vascular disease, cerebrovascular diseases, as well as many kinds of cancers. Alcohol is known to be a contributing factor to as many as 75 human diseases and conditions, most notably cirrhosis of the liver and cancer of the mouth, throat, esophagus, stomach, and liver. Heavy drinkers increase their risk of gastrointestinal disorders, heart disease, and high blood pressure. But few known mechanisms plausibly link illicit drug use to common diseases.

Admittedly, marijuana smoke is carcinogenic. But the quantity of smoke inhaled over time is the most important factor in predicting the likelihood of cancer. Since users of marijuana smoke so much less than smokers of tobacco products, it is not surprising that epidemiological statistics fail to show higher rates of cancer in smokers of marijuana.[5] Cocaine increases the risk of coronary artery disease, which is particularly worrisome for those with preexisting heart problems – but is not otherwise implicated in common physical diseases. Heavy users may experience paranoia, which includes anxiety, sleeplessness, hypertension, suspicion, and fears of persecution. But many of these same symptoms are common in alcoholics; up to 85 percent of frequent cocaine users are heavy drinkers, making the effects of the two substances difficult to disentangle. Comparable problems surround attempts to measure the health risks of opiates. Contemporary heroin addicts tend to lead a notoriously unhealthy lifestyle, eating a terrible diet, avoiding doctors, and smoking large numbers of cigarettes. But opiates themselves seem to be fairly nontoxic; addicts whose lifestyle is otherwise healthy and who have a steady supply of heroin suffer primarily from constipation but have few other difficulties.

5 The best summary of health hazards of marijuana is Mitch Earlywine, *Understanding Marijuana: A New Look at the Scientific Evidence* (New York: Oxford University Press, 2002).

Although I have contrasted the health risks of illicit drugs with those of licit drugs, we should look elsewhere – beyond drugs of any kind – to demonstrate the implausibility of using the criminal law to protect people from health risks. Many activities that do not involve the use of a drug are far more risky to health, even though no one would dream of using the criminal law to prohibit them. Melanoma, caused largely by excessive exposure to the Sun, kills more people in the United States than all illicit drugs combined. We should rethink our willingness to punish illicit drug users when told that the risks of sunbathing are greater. But unhealthy foods provide the best source of examples. Every year, according to the Center for Disease Control and Prevention, about 5,000 deaths, 325,000 hospitalizations, and 76 million illnesses are caused by food poisoning. Contamination is only a small part of the problem. More than half of all Americans are now overweight. The 100 million adults who are obese far outnumber illicit drug users, and the health hazards of excessive weight are more easily demonstrated than those of illicit drugs. According to the Center for Disease Control and Prevention, obesity may account for about 300,000 deaths a year – far more than all illicit and licit drugs (except tobacco) combined. Of course, the number of fatalities does not tell the whole story; obesity diminishes the health and quality of life in myriad ways. For example, the risk of (Type 2) diabetes increases 4 percent for every pound of excess weight. Diabetes is a major cause of blindness, kidney failure, and leg amputation and greatly increases the risk of heart disease and stroke. And diabetes is just one of the many diseases associated with obesity.

High-calorie foods that cause obesity are hardly the only examples that illustrate my point. Illicit recreational drugs do not pose significant health risks relative to any number of recreational activities that we tolerate and even applaud. Mountain climbing is a good illustration. Competitive sports such as boxing and rugby provide excellent examples as well. Mothers who would be devastated by the news that their sons are experimenting with drugs are proud to learn that their kids are playing football. But the carnage in the most decrepit crack house is less worrisome than what can be seen on football fields throughout the United States. According to a 2001 study, 65 percent of professional football players suffer a major injury while playing – that is, an injury that either requires surgery or forces them to miss at least eight games. Two of every three former professionals indicate that their injuries limit their abilities to participate in sports and other recreational activities in retirement. Of course, amateurs are severely injured as well. About one-third of all college football players suffer a concussion; one in five has more than one.[6] Even the most pessimistic estimates of the health risks of illicit drug use are far less shocking.

Of course, the issue of whether a risk should be tolerated depends partly on why people are prepared to take it. Doctors who tested experimental serums on their own body are often singled out as heroes, since the potential gains to public health are so great. But competitive sports such as rugby are played solely for recreation – for the entertainment of participants and spectators. If we seriously propose to invoke the criminal law against persons who take health risks for recreational purposes, those who play dangerous sports would have to be punished. This result, of course, would be ludicrous.

In short, no other recreational activity is singled out for severe punishment because of its risks to health. The only conceivable basis for treating illicit drugs differently from other recreational activities is that the former are more risky, by a substantial degree, than the latter. But illicit drug use is *not* more risky than any number of these behaviors. As I have said, illicit drug use is not recommended for persons whose foremost priority is health and safety. But the use of illicit drugs is not especially high on the list of health problems in the United States today.

The health considerations I have discussed in this section might persuade us that we would be foolish to elect to participate in given risky activities. As a matter of public policy, behaviors that pose significant risks to well-being should be discouraged. But

6 William Nack and Lester Munson, "The Wrecking Yard," 94 *Sports Illustrated* 60 (2001).

these considerations should not convince us to resort to criminal-ization. We should all welcome state policies to improve health. Punishments, however – especially when they are severe – are simply not an acceptable part of the equation.

Drugs and Children

The next possible answer to the fundamental question "Why should recreational users of (some) drugs be punished?" is that prohibition is justified in order to protect children. According to this rationale, the drug war is fought on behalf of America's youth. This rationale has a tremendous appeal. We all want what is best for our children. They seem to need all of the help they can get – for our children are *not* very well protected from illicit drugs at the present time. According to recent surveys,[7] almost 60 percent of high school seniors have tried an illicit drug at some point in their life; 41 percent of high school seniors and 36 percent of sopho-mores said they had used an illicit drug in the past year. More significantly, almost 33 percent of seniors are "current users" – that is, used an illicit drug within 30 days of the poll. In light of this alarming statistic, prohibitionists ask us to support what-ever policies will prevent children from succumbing to the evils of drugs.

I take this rationale seriously, but not because it is especially persuasive. Indeed, I think it is probably the *worst* of the four rea-sons to criminalize drug use that I will evaluate in this chapter. I take this rationale seriously because it is so pervasive. Images of children are conspicuous in antidrug campaigns. According to the ONDCP, the *first* objective of our drug policy is to ensure that America's youth will reject illegal drugs. Needless to say, this objective is thought to require the punishment of adult drug users.

How should we evaluate this rationale for our existing drug policy? As a preliminary point, we should avoid the use of the

7 *Sourcebook of Criminal Justice Statistics* online, Table 3.88 (http://www.albany. edu/sourcebook/pdf/t386.pdf).

word *children* as inflammatory and misleading. This word suggests that we are talking about policies to protect, say, eight-year olds. Despite the publicity and concern that surround a few notorious cases, not many "children" actually use illicit drugs. In reality, the rationale I examine here involves teenagers – those in their late teens in particular. Policies that may seem sensible to protect elementary school kids become far more dubious when applied to college sophomores. Henceforth, I will use the more appropriate term *adolescents* to describe the class of persons we are trying to protect by this rationale for criminalization.

Why is this rationale so unpersuasive? First, notice that our alleged concern for the welfare of adolescents seems to vanish as soon as they actually begin to use illicit drugs. When they are caught with drugs, sympathies are put aside and mercy is seldom forthcoming. The ONDCP promotes "zero tolerance policies for youth regarding the use of illegal drugs." There is a growing trend in criminal justice to prosecute and sentence juveniles as adults. Recent FBI figures strongly suggest that the war on drugs is becoming a war on youth. While most other crime fell dramatically during the last decade, drug arrests were up 37 percent since 1993; for teens below age 18, the increase was 59 percent, with more than 133,000 adolescents busted for drugs in 2002.[8] This trend is hard to reconcile with the image of the innocent child who needs to be protected from the dangers of drugs. Against this background, are we really to believe that our deep concern for the welfare of children justifies our policy of punishing drug users?

In addition, our aim to ensure that juveniles remain drug-free is quickly forgotten when doctors purport to detect a syndrome or disorder. Every day in North America, about 5 million kids use Ritalin, a relatively powerful psychostimulant. The United States and Canada account for about 95 percent of the consumption of Ritalin throughout the world. Many doctors do not believe that "attention deficit disorder" should be treated with drugs and denounce Ritalin as nothing more than "cocaine for kids." Of

---

8 Ibid., Table 4.7 (http://www.albany.edu/sourcebook/pdf/t17.pdf).

course, adolescents who use real cocaine without a prescription face serious criminal penalties.

Despite these skeptical observations, I do not think that this proposed rationale for selective prohibition should be brushed aside or dismissed so casually. Instead, I propose to subject it to a serious evaluation. Might the laudable objective of protecting adolescents really justify the criminalization of drug use? We should begin by asking how this objective *could* justify a policy that imprisons hundreds of thousands of Americans for using drugs. After all, the vast majority of drug users are adults. How *can* punishing adults help to protect adolescents? The answer would be clear if we believed that adults instigate the behavior we are trying to prevent. In cases in which adults are predators and children are unwilling victims – as in most cases of sexual molestation – we are and ought to be quick to resort to punishment. But drug use is hardly comparable. No one still believes that juveniles reluctantly begin to use drugs because of the pernicious encouragement of adults. The myth of the pusher, for example, has been wholly discredited. We now know that peers – friends and acquaintances, not adult drug dealers – introduce adolescents to illicit drugs. The decision to experiment with illicit drugs such as marijuana and ecstasy is not unlike the decision to try licit drugs such as tobacco and alcohol. Adult predators or pushers play no significant role here. In any event, adults could be punished in those rare cases in which they *do* encourage teens to use drugs. Most jurisdictions already punish such behavior. We could retain these laws, even without prohibiting adult drug use itself.

What, then, *is* the connection between the punishment of adults and the protection of juveniles? Frankly, the matter is unclear. But the most plausible answer, I submit, is as follows: Whenever we allow adults to do something that we prohibit for adolescents, we can anticipate what might be called *leakage*. Inevitably, some of what is available to adults will "trickle down" and find its way into the hands of our nation's youth. When we try to ban something only for adolescents, kids who are ingenious and determined will somehow succeed in getting it. As long as adults can use something without fear of punishment, we should not expect that juveniles can be effectively prevented from obtaining it. Leakage must be minimized if we really are serious about protecting teens from the dangers of drugs. The best way to do so is to punish adults as well as adolescents for using illicit drugs.

The problem of leakage occurs in any context in which we try to protect adolescents but are unwilling to resort to the punishment of adults. Violent depictions or sexual images on television and the Internet are good examples. If we really were serious about preventing leakage – about minimizing the likelihood that children will be exposed to violence or sex – we would ban these pictures for everyone. That option, however, is unacceptable. Instead, we resort to imperfect solutions. We invent devices that scramble cable signals and disable computers from accessing adult sites. We try our best to minimize leakage, without resorting to the extreme device of putting adults in jail for doing what we do not want our children to do.

We have ample evidence of leakage in the case of alcohol and tobacco. Adolescents frequently obtain their supplies of alcohol and tobacco through lawful purchases by adults. Some adults willingly share their supplies with underage drinkers and smokers; other teens obtain alcohol or tobacco from adults surreptitiously. If we were as determined to prevent juveniles from using tobacco or alcohol as we are to prevent them from using illicit drugs, we would punish adults who smoke or drink in the way we punish them for using illicit drugs. Of course, we do not punish adults who smoke or drink. Despite the anxiety we feel about underage smokers and drinkers, no one seriously proposes that we minimize leakage by resorting to this drastic measure. Instead of punishing adults, we employ other strategies to limit leakage. We take elaborate precautions to restrict direct sales to kids and require purchasers to show proof of age. These safeguards are helpful but flawed; no one pretends they are more than marginally effective. Our measures are easily circumvented, and considerable leakage of licit drugs takes place.

According to the rationale I propose to evaluate here, punishment is justified as a way to prevent the leakage to adolescents that would occur if illicit drug use were decriminalized for adults. I will argue that we have at least four reasons to reject this rationale for criminalization. First, I will contend that this rationale provides a much better reason to punish drug production and sale than to punish use. Second, I will show that we do not effectively prevent leakage, despite our willingness to punish adults. Third, I will maintain that our efforts to reduce leakage often do more harm than good to the very juveniles we are trying to protect. Finally and most controversially, I will argue that the evils of drugs to adolescents are not sufficiently grave to justify the enormous price we pay in trying to prevent leakage.

First, this rationale for prohibition would be more plausible if we assume that decriminalization must extend to drug production and sale. Any lawful system of drug distribution might well increase leakage to adolescents. But decriminalization, as I have defined it here, applies only to illicit drug *use*. How would the failure to punish drug users increase leakage? A change in the laws that punish users need not increase supplies of drugs at all. Unless greater supplies of drugs became available, it is hard to see why we should anticipate that greater amounts of drugs would turn up in the hands of teens. *Perhaps* a bit more leakage might occur if we stopped punishing drug users. The failure to punish users might stimulate the demand for drugs; greater demand might lead to an increase in supply, which might facilitate leakage. But this explanation of why decriminalization might cause leakage is far less plausible than a scenario in which we imagine that adolescents are able to fabricate their identification or break into stores in which legalized drugs are lawfully bought and sold. As long as production and sale are still prohibited, decriminalization might allow us to prevent leakage as effectively as we do today.

Or, rather, as *ineffectively* as we do today. The second reason to reject this rationale for punishing recreational users of illicit drugs is that it fails to accomplish its goal – prevention of a substantial amount of leakage. Since adults are willing and able to obtain illicit drugs, leakage to adolescents is bound to occur, despite our massive efforts to curtail it. The most telling indication of failure is the availability of illicit drugs, rather than the number of adolescents who succumb to them. In 1999, more than 56 percent of adolescents between the ages of 12 and 17 said that illicit drugs were "easy to obtain." Eighty-nine percent of high school seniors said that marijuana is "fairly easy" or "very easy" to find. Generally, they report that the difficulty of acquiring illicit drugs is comparable to that of obtaining alcohol or tobacco – for which we do not resort to punishing adults. Prohibitionists tend to respond to these reports by saying that we need to try harder, and to redouble our determination to punish adult users. But more than 30 years of warlike efforts have not proved effective in keeping drugs out of the hands of adolescents who want to get them. Why think that we will succeed tomorrow, when we have failed yesterday and today? Notice that the number of adolescents who report that drugs are easy to obtain is far greater – nearly four times greater – than the number who actually use them regularly. The great majority of adolescents do not use drugs, but not because they cannot find them.

Our punitive policies probably succeed in preventing *some* leakage to adolescents. Admittedly, a number of adolescents did *not* say that illicit drugs were easy to obtain. Drugs may take a bit more time and effort to locate because they are not freely available to adults. We cannot predict how much more leakage would occur if drug use were decriminalized. More importantly, we need to inquire *how much* more leakage would have to take place before we should proclaim criminalization to be justified. Even steadfast supporters of our punitive policies should regard this question as difficult. We sometimes talk as though we should approve of punishment if it succeeds in preventing a single teenager from succumbing to the evils of drugs. Such extreme rhetoric cannot be taken seriously. We could easily make a far more dramatic improvement in the welfare of adolescents with only a tiny fraction of the resources we allocate to drug prohibition.

How much leakage *do* we prevent? Again, we do not know. Prohibitionists may be encouraged by the substantial decrease in the use of illicit drugs among adolescents over the past 25 years. Although recent statistics about the extent of drug use among adolescents may seem to be alarming, we need to be reminded of the progress that has been made. In 1979, the year of peak drug use in the United States, about 25 million youths were current users of illicit drugs. But these findings do not really provide much basis for believing that our punitive drug policies are successful in preventing significant amounts of leakage. Over the same period, the use of alcohol among adolescents has declined as well. In 1979, nearly 50 percent of 12- to 17-year-olds reported drinking at some point in the previous month; now that figure is barely 20 percent.[9] Many factors explain this downward trend in the consumption of alcohol among adolescents. Obviously, however, an increase in our willingness to punish adult drinkers cannot be among these factors. Evidently, substantial reductions in drug use among adolescents can be (and have been) produced without resorting to the extreme measure of incarcerating adults.

We have a third reason to reject this rationale for criminalization. Even if our policy prevents some amount of leakage, this alleged justification for punishing drug users is persuasive only if it achieves a net gain in the welfare of adolescents. No one endorses a cure that is worse than a disease. Parents desperately want what is best for their kids; they want to prevent them from using drugs. As we have seen, however, millions of adolescents stubbornly persist, notwithstanding our efforts. What is best for these teens? We can gain a perspective on this question by asking what a parent should be worried about when he or she suspects or learns that his son or daughter is taking drugs. Two very different kinds of answers might be given. First, the parent might be concerned about the effects of the drugs. Second, he or she might fear that a son or daughter will be arrested and punished. Which fear is greater? For the vast majority of adolescents who use drugs, the second concern is more worrisome than the first. As we will see, the effects of drugs on adolescents are likely to be minimal and temporary. But the effects of punishment are often

9 Substance Abuse and Mental Health Services Administration, *The 1998 National Household Survey on Drug Abuse* (Washington, DC: Samhsa, 1999), Table 14. Subsequent results have countinued this trend.

substantial and lasting. Among the worst things we can do to adolescents is to turn them into criminals and to punish them. And we *have* been punishing them – at an alarming rate. In 1986, 31 of every 100,000 adolescents were incarcerated for drug offenses. By 1996, 122 of every 100,000 were sent to prison for drug offenses – a 391 percent increase. If we really are so concerned about the welfare of the next generation, we should not be eager to punish so many of them.

Parents who demand that drug users should be imprisoned in order to protect adolescents rarely consider the very real possibility that their *own* teens will be sent to jail as a result of the policies they endorse. Every parent should be made to answer the question "Suppose *your* son or daughter is caught using drugs. How much time do you think he or she should spend in jail?" We approve of punishing your kids to protect my kids, but feel altogether differently when my kids are punished to protect yours. Some parents have learned this lesson the hard way. The realization that punishment is the more serious danger to adolescents has contributed to the formation of groups like Families against Mandatory Minimums (FAMM).

We want to help our kids, but we do not always know how to do it. One thing we *do* know is that punishing parents who use drugs is very bad for their sons and daughters – the very kids we are trying to protect. Suppose a parent uses drugs and is not as good a parent as she or he otherwise might be. Can we seriously believe that the welfare of the family is enhanced if we throw that drug-using parent into jail? Juveniles whose parents are imprisoned are far more likely to become criminals themselves. The terrible effects on adolescents are especially acute when their mother is punished. Drug prohibition has made women – and mothers in particular – the fastest growing segment of the prison population. Women now make up about 6 percent of all persons incarcerated – more than twice the rate of 1978. Less than 15 percent of these women were imprisoned for crimes of violence. In all other contexts, our concern for the welfare of children leads us to try very hard to ensure that families remain intact. But prohibitionists do not hesitate to tear families apart in the guise of protecting children.

So far, I have argued that prohibition does not prevent much leakage to adolescents and probably causes them a net balance of harm. If I am correct, we have sufficient reason to reject this alleged justification for punishing drug users. But we have a final reason to reject this rationale as well – a reason that is far more controversial than the preceding three. We must confront the most difficult question raised by this rationale: Is it really so crucial that we protect adolescents from drugs? This objective had better be of supreme importance, or it could not possibly justify the warlike effort that is waged in order to achieve it. We should examine more carefully exactly why we are so intent on trying to keep these substances away from adolescents. How bad *are* drugs for underage users?

How should we try to get a handle on this question? *Longitudinal studies* provide the best possible evidence about the effects of drugs on adolescents. These studies track persons who used drugs as adolescents over long periods, both before and after their drug-consuming years. Longitudinal studies offer valuable data about how drugs came to affect the life of those adults who had used them during their adolescent years. What do these longitudinal studies reveal about the life of individuals who took drugs as adolescents? Not surprisingly, these effects vary enormously. The life of most adults was relatively unaffected; that of a small minority was devastated. Fortunately (for research purposes), however, tens of millions of Americans who now are middle-aged used illicit drugs throughout their adolescence. In general, how do such persons fare relative to a control group of adults of the same age who did not use drugs? If illicit drug use were really so bad for adolescents, one would expect that those who used them would turn out significantly worse as adults than comparably aged individuals who abstained. But the studies do not confirm this expectation.

In the best such studies, young children are given batteries of tests to identify their psychological health.[10] They are asked the

---

10 The most well-known of the several longitudinal studies of drug users is Jonathan Shedler and Jack Block, "Adolescent Drug Use and Psychological Health," 45 *American Psychologist* 612 (1990).

following sorts of questions: Do they believe themselves to be happy? Do they regard themselves as attractive and successful? Are they moody or violent? Are they able to control their temper? These same subjects are tested again and again – usually, at three-year intervals. When they become adolescents, some but not all begin to use illicit drugs. Subjects then are placed in three categories: abstainers, experimenters, or frequent users. Most adolescents fall into one of the first two categories; few are heavy users. By the time they become young adults, most of these subjects have stopped using illicit drugs – an important point to which I will return. Subjects again are given standard psychological tests of well-being; a number of appropriate questions are added. How frequently have they changed jobs? Or been divorced? How much money do they earn? Have they had trouble paying their bills? Their answers to these (and many other similar) questions are tracked over time.

Longitudinal tests reveal that adults who had experimented with illicit drugs tend to be the best adjusted of the three groups. These individuals score high on standard tests of psychological health. Adults who had been heavy drug users tend to be the least well off. Many such individuals are maladjusted and alienated, exhibiting poor impulse control and emotional distress. Adults who had been abstainers tend to fall between the two extremes. Their overall psychological state is better than that of heavy drug users, but worse than that of experimenters. Although these sorts of studies must be evaluated carefully, they tend to show that moderate recreational drug use among adolescents is no cause for alarm. This finding is absolutely crucial for purposes of evaluating this rationale for our drug policy. It provides the basis for my claim that a concerned parent should be less worried about how drugs will affect his or her child than about the possibility of arrest and prosecution. Anyone who proposes to punish adult users in order to prevent leakage to adolescents should be prepared to reconsider this rationale in light of the fact that the great majority of drug-using adolescents do not suffer in the long run.

Middle-aged parents should be skeptical of the claim that criminalization is required to protect their children. They must be aware that the drugs they consumed in their youth did not ruin their life. Parents who used drugs as adolescents somehow managed to survive the ordeal. Still, these same parents are often persuaded that we should imprison those who do today what they did not so long ago. Why do they believe this? They cannot think that their own life would have been improved if they had been thrown into jail. Sometimes, they are led to believe that the drugs of today are unlike the drugs they took during their adolescence. The drugs now available are said to be more potent, and therefore more dangerous, than those consumed a generation ago. Most of these claims are demonstrably false. Although some kinds of drugs tend to be somewhat more potent today than a generation ago, other kinds of drugs – such as LSD – are less so. And higher potency is not always bad. In the case of marijuana, an increase in potency (measured by higher THC content) might actually prove beneficial. The primary health hazards of marijuana derive from the fact that it is smoked. Risks increase with the quantity, rather than with the potency of what is smoked. The greater the potency, the less that is needed to reach the same psychological state. The same is true of heroin. Higher potencies have contributed to the recent trend of smoking rather than injecting heroin, which minimizes the risks of AIDS and hepatitis – health hazards far greater than the effects of heroin itself.

I do not pretend that the foregoing observations will put to rest all of our fears about drugs and kids. These anxieties will always remain with us. Adolescents will continue to engage in behaviors that alarm their parents. They stay up late, eat junk foods, have sex (frequently unprotected), study too little, skip school, pierce their body, play extreme sports, incur too much debt, succumb to peer pressure, and the like. But the extent of these risks should not be exaggerated. We must be sufficiently mature and honest to admit that some problems will never be completely solved. In any event, our punitive drug policies cannot possibly be justified in order to protect our sons and daughters from the evils of drugs. In no other context would we approve of a policy that prevented adults from engaging in a type of activity simply because it was bad for children. This rationale for criminalization treats adults *as* children – that is, *as though* they are children. I have argued that punishing adults for this purpose is ineffective and causes great harm to those it purports to protect. Finally, I have suggested that drug use, even among adolescents, does not appear to be sufficiently destructive to justify the punishment of adults in our futile effort to prevent it.

Drugs and Crime

Rates of violent crime in the United States are unacceptably high. Still, enormous progress has recently been made. The country has experienced a significant reduction in crime throughout the last decade. Experts disagree about why. Possible answers include overall economic prosperity, an aging population with fewer adolescents, better police work, longer sentences for violent criminals, more effective precautions by citizens and the private sector, and even the availability of safe and legal abortions (which prevented unwanted children who might have become criminals from being born). Another possible answer is the strict enforcement of laws that punish drug users. "Drug control is crime control," proclaims Rudolph Guiliani, former mayor of New York City. The goal of reducing violent crime provides the third of the four possible answers to the fundamental question I will evaluate in this chapter. According to the ONDCP, the most important objective of our drug policy – after the protection of children – is to "increase the safety of America's citizens by substantially reducing drug-related crime and violence." In this section, I will critically respond to the rationale that crime prevention justifies our policy of punishing people who use illicit drugs for recreational purposes.

This rationale can be contested on empirical grounds. Our willingness to punish illicit drug users may do little to explain the recent decline in rates of violent crime. Whether increases in the punishment of drug users coincide with decreases in violent crime depends on the year we choose as the baseline of comparison. In the 1990s, crime plummeted while punishments for drug use soared. Suppose, however, that we adopt a somewhat longer perspective and examine these phenomena since 1980. Our prison population has tripled 250 percent since 1980 – much of that, as we have seen, due to greater punishments for drug users. Yet we now have about the same level of nondrug crime as we had then. If the punishment of drug users really were an effective means to reduce violent crime, one would expect that an increase in the former would be correlated more closely with a decrease in the latter over longer periods.

Moreover, we should insist on getting the correct statistics before confidently proclaiming that drug use causes crime. Prohibitionists often point out that a high percentage of criminals test positive for illicit drugs. In England, Phil Wheatley, director general of the Prison Service, reported in 2002 that 80 percent of prisoners test positive for illicit drugs when they begin their sentence. What should we conclude from this fact? The percentage of criminals who are drug users is not as meaningful as the percentage of drug users who are criminals. The latter percentage, after all, is extraordinarily low. Those who believe that drug use causes crime must struggle to explain why the vast majority of drug users never engage in violent conduct.

Empirical misgivings aside, I am more interested in assessing whether this rationale is acceptable from the perspective of justice. In a just state, *should* we allow drug users to be punished in order to reduce violent crime? Initially, we might be tempted to answer affirmatively. In principle, crime reduction is probably the *best* rationale for punishing illicit drug users. Everyone understands the importance of reducing violent crime. Many criminal laws that almost certainly are justified – those that punish attempts, for example – are designed to prevent serious crime *before* it happens. Laws prohibiting drug use might be justified if they serve this same purpose. If we really succeed in preventing significant amounts of crime by punishing illicit drug users, how could any reasonable person believe that these punishments are not justified?

To evaluate this rationale, we must look more carefully at *how* and *why* the punishment of recreational drug users might reduce violent crime. In other words, we must try to understand the nature of the *drug–crime connection*. This topic is extraordinarily complex. Fortunately, social scientists have developed very powerful frameworks for understanding the link between drugs and crime.[11] At least three types of crimes might be linked to drug use. The first types of crimes are *systemic*. These crimes occur because illicit drugs are bought and sold in black markets. When something goes wrong with illicit drug production or sale, buyers and sellers do not have the redress that we take for granted when a problem arises with a lawful product. If a seller cheats a buyer, or if a consumer refuses to pay a dealer, the complaining party can hardly go to the courthouse to file a lawsuit. Disputes of this sort must be resolved outside normal legal channels. As a result, one would expect that illicit drug markets would be violent. Our history appears to confirm this expectation. Black markets were notoriously violent during the era of alcohol prohibition. Today, the black market in cocaine is comparable. The systemic crimes associated with illicit drugs include highly publicized cases of murder due to disputes involving illegal drug transactions. Sometimes, innocent children are killed in gun battles between rival drug gangs. These tragedies always give rise to calls for stricter enforcement of existing drug laws. Paradoxically, stricter enforcement can make dealing more profitable, thereby increasing the incidence of the very systemic crimes it is designed to prevent.

Without question, much of the violent crime associated with illicit drugs is systemic. By most estimates, this category accounts for about 75 percent of drug-related crime. Decriminalization would reduce the incidence of these systemic crimes. Of course, systemic crime would be *drastically* reduced if decriminalization were extended beyond drug use to include drug production and sale. Even opponents of legalization do not always predict that it would lead to a net increase in crime. Despite his enthusiasm for prohibition, James Q. Wilson writes: "It is not clear that enforcing the laws against drug use would reduce crime. On the contrary,

---

11 The classic source is Paul Goldstein, "The Drug/Violence Nexus: A Tripartite Conceptual Framework," 14 *Journal of Drug Issues* 493 (1985).

crime may be caused by such enforcement."[12] According to this school of thought, an overall increase in crime is the price we must be willing to pay for the several advantages we gain by laws that prohibit drug use.

In my judgment, Wilson is half right and half wrong. He is probably correct to think that more crime, rather than less, is caused by our prohibition of drug use. He is incorrect, however, to conclude that the advantage that such laws allegedly produce – a decrease in the incidence of drug use – outweighs this disadvantage. I believe that the enormous amount of systemic crime caused by prohibition is too high a price to pay for any of the speculative goods that might result from punishing drug users. Unfortunately, I cannot *prove* that I am correct about how these advantages and disadvantages should be balanced. But I would bet that the innocent victims of systemic crimes would tend to agree with my assessment that the drawbacks outweigh the benefits. The mother of an innocent child killed in a confrontation between drug dealers and the police would be stunned to learn that serious academics concede that legalization would have saved the life of her child but oppose it nonetheless.

Clearly, decriminalization would reduce the amount of systemic crime. This recognition puts us in a better position to decide whether selective prohibition can be justified as a means to prevent crime. The disputed and crucial issue is not simply whether drug use causes crime, but whether drug use causes criminal conduct that would persist even if drug use itself were not prohibited. When we try to assess the merits of decriminalization by analyzing the drug–crime connection, we should remember that most criminal behavior associated with drugs is not caused by drugs per se, but rather by the fact that drug use is illegal.

This crucial point must be kept in mind as we turn our attention to the second type of crime associated with illicit drugs: *economic* crime. Drug use causes economic crime for a simple reason. Partly because of addiction, many illicit drug users want

12 James Q. Wilson, "Drugs and Crime," in Michael Tonry and James Q. Wilson, eds., *Drugs and Crime* (Chicago: University of Chicago Press, 1990), p. 522.

drugs very badly and are willing to go to extraordinary lengths to obtain them. Many illicit drugs are expensive. This combination of strong demand and high price leads users to commit economic crimes to get the money to buy drugs. Some estimates of the number of property offenses committed by drug addicts are astronomical.

Whatever the true extent of economic crime associated with illicit drugs, we must struggle to determine whether such crime is caused by drugs, or is caused by drug prohibitions. If less economic crime would occur under decriminalization, the goal of reducing economic crime could hardly be the rationale for punishing drug users. Unfortunately, this question is not easy to answer. Again, the main difficulty is our lack of certainty about how illicit drugs would be bought and sold if drug users were no longer punished. Under most models of legalized markets, illicit drugs would be less expensive. Some academics have estimated that heroin could be lawfully bought and sold at about 2 percent of its current, black-market price. If this estimate were roughly accurate, one would anticipate that legalizing the sale of heroin (and other illicit drugs) would cause a drastic reduction in economic crime. This prediction is based partly on an examination of the extent of economic crime associated with licit drugs. Alcoholics and tobacco addicts rarely steal to purchase their drugs, but not because their addictions are less powerful. Instead, these addicts can typically afford to buy what users of illicit drugs cannot.

On the other hand, as I will explain in more detail in Chapter 5, drugs in legalized markets may *not* be significantly less expensive. The price of these drugs would depend on unknown variables such as the rate of taxation. In addition, if legalized drugs were really less expensive, greater numbers of people might be temped to use them. Greater numbers of users might translate into a higher population of addicts, who in turn might cause greater amounts of economic crime – even though drugs were cheaper. No one should be very confident about how the incidence of economic crime would be affected by changes in our punitive drug policies. Despite this uncertainty, one point is clear. The incidence of economic crime associated with illicit drugs is not simply attributable to illicit drugs per se, but to complex features of drug markets – most notably, to the high price of drugs. High prices are due more to the fact that drug sales are illegal than to the cost of producing illicit drugs. If our objective is the reduction of economic crime, we are better off controlling markets and fixing the price of illicit drugs at the point at which the incidence of economic crime is minimized. There is no reason to believe that this optimal point corresponds to the cost of drugs in the black markets of today. We should be very reluctant to believe that punishing drug users is an effective way to reduce economic crime.

The third type of crime in the drug–crime connection is *psychopharmacological*. This category of crime results from the effects of drugs themselves, rather than from the fact that their use and sale are prohibited. Experts disagree about the causal mechanisms that might lead some drug users to become violent. Drugs may release inhibitions that can generally be restrained. Or drugs may impair judgment and perception, leading users to act unpredictably. According to William Bennett, "The fact is that under the influence of drugs, normal people do not act normally, and abnormal people behave in chilling and horrible ways."[13] This account of the connection between drug use and crime is reminiscent of the story of Dr. Jekyll and Mr. Hyde. Dr. Jekyll consumed a potion that transformed him into the homicidal Mr. Hyde. The psychopharmacological effects of this potion caused an otherwise law-abiding physician to become a violent monster. Of course, this story is purely fictitious. If any existing drug resembled the potion in this story, we would have excellent reasons to criminalize its use.

Fortunately, no existing drug resembles this imaginary potion. Scholars are far more ambivalent than Bennett about this explanation of the drug–crime connection. Research provides no evidence that people under the influence of marijuana or heroin are

---

13 William Bennett, "The Plea to Legalize Drugs Is a Siren Call to Surrender," in Michael Lyman and Gary Potter, eds., *Drugs in Society* (Cincinnati: Anderson, 1991), p. 338.

more likely to become aggressive and violent. These drugs tend to have the opposite effect; their psychopharmacological properties cause users to become passive. Studies indicate that users of marijuana are *under*represented among violent criminals when researchers are careful to control for other variables such as age. The situation with cocaine is a bit less clear. Cocaine users themselves, however, seldom report that the drug leads them to commit violent acts they would not have performed otherwise. Ironically, alcohol is the drug most likely to lead to psychopharmacological crime. If we accept this rationale for punishing drug users – and prohibit those drugs that cause people to become violent and aggressive – we would begin by punishing drinkers. More generally, if we propose to ban those drugs that are implicated in criminal behavior, no drug would be a better candidate for criminalization than alcohol. In 1998, the National Center on Addiction and Substance Abuse (NCASA) reported that 21 percent of persons in state jails or prisons for violent crime were under the influence of alcohol and no other drug at the time they committed their crime. Only 3 percent were under the influence of cocaine or crack alone; a mere 1 percent were under the influence of heroin alone.

Alcohol aside, we cannot justify the punishment of drug users in order to prevent systemic, economic, or psychopharmacological crime. In fact, a growing number of scholars believe that punishing drug use actually causes more crime in lower-class neighborhoods than it prevents. After all, incarcerated drug users will have to be released and returned to their community *sometime*. Although the Supreme Court has ruled that lifetime imprisonment is not an unconstitutionally severe sentence for the crime of cocaine possession, no one really proposes to keep drug users behind bars indefinitely. Because of the long sentences imposed on them, drug users who are released are less likely to find employment or housing or to reestablish ties with their family. As a result, they are more likely to resort to criminality – and not merely crimes involving drugs. Nearly one-fifth of all persons locked up for nonviolent offenses are eventually rearrested for violent crimes. Although criminalization can produce short-term benefits, it may cause an increase in crime in the long run.

My conclusion is simple: No account of the drug–crime connection provides an acceptable justification for criminalizing drug use.

Drugs and Immorality

Arguably, the foregoing discussions miss the point of drug prohibitions. Perhaps the best rationale for criminalization does not depend on the *effects* or *consequences* of illicit drugs in contributing to disease or illness, harming adolescents, or causing crime. Instead, punishing drug users might be defensible as a *moral* imperative. William Bennett writes: "I find no merit in the legalizers' case. The simple fact is that drug use is wrong. And the moral argument, in the end, is the most compelling argument."[14] Barry McAffrey, the subsequent drug czar, concurs. President Bush remarks that "legalizing drugs would completely undermine the message that drug use is wrong."[15] James Q. Wilson expresses this view eloquently:

> Even now, when the dangers of drug use are well-understood, many educated people still discuss the drug problem in almost every way except the right way. They talk about the "costs" of drug use and the "socioeconomic factors" that shape that use. They rarely speak plainly – drug use is wrong because it is immoral and it is immoral because it enslaves the mind and destroys the soul.[16]

As we will see, most people in the United States appear to agree with this moral judgment.

This final rationale for prohibition can be expressed as a *syllogism* – that is, as an argument containing two premises and a conclusion. Although this argument admits of several variations, its most straightforward version is as follows: According to the

14 Ibid., p. 339.
15 Remarks by President Bush in announcing the new head of the Office of the National Drug Control Policy, May 10, 2001.
16 See William Bennett, John Dilulio, Jr., and John Walters, *Body Count* (New York: Simon & Schuster, 1996), pp. 140–1.

first premise of the argument (the major premise), *the criminal law should punish people who behave immorally*. According to the second premise (the minor premise), *illicit drug use for recreational purposes is immoral*. If these two premises were true, the conclusion of the syllogism would be irresistible: *The criminal law should punish people who use illicit drugs for recreational purposes*. In this section, I will try to show why this syllogism is unsound and fails to provide a persuasive rationale for criminalization. I will argue against both the major and the minor premise of this alleged justification for punishing drug users. I will conclude by suggesting that prohibitionists, rather than those who use drugs, are guilty of the more egregious immorality.

Many legal philosophers would dismiss this rationale out of hand because they reject its major premise: that the criminal law should punish people who behave immorally. This premise is called *legal moralism*. Those who oppose legal moralism do not believe that the criminal law should punish people for immoral behavior. They differ in their reasons for rejecting legal moralism. A few of these theorists claim to be able to make no sense of morality at all, contending it to be a superstition or illusion. No one thinks that we should punish people for reasons that are only superstitions. Most legal philosophers, however, admit that morality makes sense. They agree that the immorality of behavior is relevant to the case for criminalization. After all, the immorality of murder, rape, and theft is central to the justification for punishing these acts. These wrongful activities are criminalized because they harm victims and violate their moral rights. But most legal philosophers insist that immorality is only *necessary*, not *sufficient* for criminalization. In other words, something in addition to immoral behavior is needed before punishment is justified.

These theorists point out that our system of criminal justice makes no effort to punish every instance of immoral behavior – even those that are more clearly immoral than drug use. We do not punish those who lie to their friends, cheat on their exams, or are openly unfaithful to their spouse. I will focus on only one of many possible examples of immorality that is not criminalized – breaches of contract. Suppose that one party deliberately breaks a promise to another that is written in a solemn, binding contract. Parties who break their contractual promises can be sued and ordered to pay monetary damages, but they do not commit crimes for which they can be prosecuted and sent to prison. No one thinks that the law should be changed so that we can begin to punish parties who break their contractual agreements. Yet there is little or no dispute that breaking these promises is immoral. Therefore, no one seems to think that *all* immoral conduct should be punished by the criminal law. Apparently, only *some* immoral conduct should be punished. If so, prohibitionists who contend that drug use should be punished because of its immorality should be pressed to explain why *this* case, unlike a case of breaking a contractual promise, should be included among those immoral behaviors the criminal law should punish. Perhaps the rationales I have already examined are attempts to provide such a reason. For example, we might decide to criminalize those cases of immorality that threaten adolescents, increase the risk of crime, or jeopardize our health. But mere immorality, without more, should not be punished. Legal moralism, which allows punishment simply for immorality, should be rejected as a persuasive rationale for criminalization.

I conclude that we should reject this first premise in the latest rationale for criminalization. If I am correct, the entire rationale should be rejected; we need only oppose one premise in a syllogism to resist its conclusion. If we reject legal moralism, any controversy surrounding the second, minor premise becomes moot. We can concede that recreational drug use is immoral, while denying that this concession provides a rationale for criminalization. But I think we should go further. We must offer a reason to reject this syllogism that should persuade even those few legal philosophers who accept legal moralism – that is, a reason that should convince those who believe that the criminal law *should* punish immorality. To my mind, the second premise in this syllogism is even less plausible than the first. In other words, I see no reason to believe that the recreational use of illicit drugs is immoral. Of course, I may be mistaken in my belief; debates about morality are notoriously hard to resolve. My seeing no reason to believe that the recreational use of illicit drugs is immoral does not show that no such reason exists. Before this second premise should be accepted as a good reason to punish drug users, we must evaluate the reasons that lead many people to conclude that recreational drug use is immoral.

What *are* these reasons? How *can* the mere act of taking a substance be immoral? This question raises perhaps the most divisive question about contemporary drug policy. Unfortunately, those who are convinced that the recreational use of illicit drugs is immoral almost never try to answer it. That is, they rarely offer a reason in support of their vehement moral condemnation of illicit drug use. Many prohibitionists apparently regard this belief as obvious or self-evident. Clearly, this sort of response – or lack of response – gets us nowhere. As long as beliefs about the immorality of drug use are not defended, we have no way to reply to people who disagree or are undecided and do not regard these beliefs as obvious or self-evident.

Why is the recreational use of illicit drugs thought to be immoral? Demands for a defense of this moral belief are perfectly reasonable. After all, we are not talking about what might be called personal or private morality, as when we say that I have my morality, and you have yours. We are talking about the kind of morality that provides a basis for punishing others – even those who do not share the same moral beliefs as the people who punish them. When morality is cited as a basis for criminalization, legal moralists typically have no difficulty in defending their beliefs about the immorality of the acts they punish. Murder, rape, and robbery are immoral because they violate rights and severely harm victims. All persons have moral rights to life, personal security, and property; acts that violate these rights are clearly immoral. But this defense, we should recall, is not available to prohibitionists who allege that recreational drug use is immoral. Recreational drug users need not harm or violate the rights of anyone. If recreational drug use is indeed immoral, we need a different reason for this belief than is available in the case of these familiar and uncontroversial crimes.

Sometimes, prohibitionists appeal to public opinion polls to try to support their belief that the recreational use of illicit drugs is immoral.[17] They point to surveys that indicate that roughly two-thirds of Americans agree that illicit drug use is morally wrong. Sixty-four percent say that marijuana use is morally wrong. Seventy-six percent report that they would continue to oppose the legalization of cocaine and heroin, even if they could be guaranteed that it would lead to less crime. This latter statistic suggests that public resistance to decriminalization may derive more from morality than from any of the rationales I have examined in the previous sections of this chapter.

For at least three reasons, however, public opinion polls fail to show that the recreational use of illicit drugs is immoral and should be punished. The first point is the most obvious. Moral controversies simply cannot be resolved by surveys. We could make no sense of the claim that the majority might be mistaken about morality if disputes of this kind could be resolved by a poll. Next, we should not be surprised to learn that the answers respondents give to pollsters are greatly affected by exactly how the question is phrased. When people are asked whether they believe that drug use is immoral, they may think that they are being asked about what I have called personal or private morality – about what they believe is right or wrong *for them*. Respondents are less likely to judge that *others* behave immorally when they use drugs. They are even less likely to say that other people deserve to be *punished* when they act wrongfully by using drugs. Only 51 percent say both that the use of marijuana is morally wrong and that it should not be tolerated.

Finally and most controversially, I think we are entitled to draw exactly the opposite conclusion from these surveys. We had better have a very powerful consensus about the immorality of given kinds of behavior before we should feel confident about punishing those who disagree with us. Legal moralists are not hesitant

17 See the 47 surveys described by Robert J. Blendon and John T. Young, "The Public and the War on Illicit Drugs," *Journal of the American Medical Association* 827 (1998).

to punish murderers, rapists, and robbers, since no one defends the moral permissibility of these acts. But 49 percent of American respondents do *not* agree with the statement that all illicit drug use is morally wrong and intolerable. About 14 percent of Americans believe that all drugs should be legalized. A recent ABC News poll found that 69 percent of adults in the United States say they would favor state laws that require treatment instead of incarceration for first and second nonviolent drug offenses. No other crime – at least no other crime enforced with such severe punishments – gives rise to such disagreement and ambivalence in the public. When significant numbers dissent, we should entertain the possibility that the majority might be mistaken and the minority might be correct. Prohibitionists who defend criminalization because polls reveal drug use to be immoral should feel embarrassed rather than vindicated when the data reveal the extent to which our citizenry is so deeply divided.

So our question remains: Why should we believe that the recreational use of illicit drugs is immoral? Sometimes, prohibitionists offer historical explanations. They remind Americans of our puritan legacy, of our longstanding suspicion of pleasure and fun, of our alleged "hedonism taboo."[18] But how are these points supposed to advance our inquiry? They cannot be taken seriously as a *justification* for criminalization. Whatever may have been true at an earlier period in our history, no one continues to believe that an activity is immoral simply because it produces pleasure. No one denounces other activities as wrongful – spectator sports and television, for example – on the ground that they are recreational. As I will argue in Chapter 4, the value of recreation provides a better basis to *defend* than to *condemn* the morality of illicit drug use.

No defense has yet been provided for the minor premise in our syllogism. In other words, we have found no reason to believe that the recreational use of (some) drugs is immoral. Where, then, do we stand with respect to this fourth and final rationale

---

18 For an instructive history, see Alan Hunt, *Governing Morals: A Social History of Moral Regulation* (Cambridge: Cambridge University Press, 1999).

for selective prohibition? Before proceeding, let me clarify my position in two respects. First, I am not saying that no sensible moral objections have ever been raised against recreational drug use. Instead, I am saying that the *kinds* of moral objections that are plausible provide a poor rationale for criminalization. Let me explain. In my judgment, the most serious moral questions about recreational drug use invoke a conception of human virtue. Philosophers have long disagreed about the details of a theory of human excellence. Greek philosophers and Christian theologians, for example, have offered very different accounts of perfection in human beings. All philosophers, however, agree that the ideal person cultivates his or her physical and intellectual talents. Drug use, especially when excessive, undermines this aspiration; these users tend to make less of their life than they might. Heavy drug use might be described as a *handicap*. Those who use drugs excessively for an extended period are destined to fall short of an ideal. According to this school of thought, heavy drug use is a moral *vice* – the opposite of a virtue.

Whether *all* recreational drug use is a vice is far more controversial. Philosophers who develop accounts of human excellence disagree about the extent to which the pursuit of pleasure is consistent with the attainment of virtue. Notwithstanding ascetic accounts that condemn all pleasurable activities, I see no reason to believe that those who aspire to perfection cannot indulge in recreational activities at least occasionally. *Perhaps* recreational drug use, unlike other recreational pursuits, is incompatible with virtue. But this claim needs to be defended rather than assumed.

In any event, the difficulty with this kind of moral position should be evident. No one seriously proposes to criminalize all vice. It is one thing to say that we deserve to be punished when we behave immorally, but quite another to say that we deserve to be punished when we handicap ourselves or fall short of an ideal. Sloth and gluttony are at odds with the development of our physical and intellectual talents, but almost all of us would be subject to punishment if these vices were criminalized. A moralistic rationale for criminalization must show that drug use is *wrongful* – not merely that it is contrary to virtue or excellence. The criminal law establishes a floor beneath which we are not permitted to sink, rather than a ceiling to which we are required to aspire.

A second clarification is needed. I am not insisting that no good reason *can* be given for concluding that the recreational use of illicit drugs is immoral. Again, a negative is notoriously hard to prove. I am only saying that no good reason *has* been given in support of this conclusion. Here, as elsewhere, the case for criminalization has not been made. I invite and encourage those prohibitionists who believe that illicit drug use is immoral to rise to the challenge and provide a good reason why we should share their belief. Until such a reason is given, even confirmed legal moralists should be unwilling to punish recreational users of illicit drugs.

Are there any reasons to believe that the recreational use of illicit drugs is *not* immoral? I think so. After all, almost no one believes that the recreational use of *all* drugs is immoral. Recall that prohibition is selective. Few of us believe that people behave immorally when they use alcohol, caffeine, or tobacco products. Moral condemnation is generally reserved for those drugs that are illicit. Is there a relevant difference between those drugs that morality permits and those that morality (allegedly) prohibits? If not, we have good reason to suspect that these objections to illicit drugs are an unfounded prejudice masquerading as a moral argument. We must inquire: From a moral point of view, is there good reason to distinguish between the use of licit and illicit drugs?

I suspect that most attempts to answer this question will rehearse one of the other rationales for criminalization I have already critiqued. In other words, those who believe that the recreational use of *illicit* drugs is immoral but condone the recreational use of *licit* drugs generally try to distinguish between the two kinds of substances by claiming that the former are especially dangerous for adolescents, linked to crime, or risky to health. If this answer is given, we do not really have a new rationale for criminalization – a rationale that is different from those discussed. The rationale appears to be new because it is couched in moral language. In fact, however, it simply uses moral language to express one of the rationales for criminalization we have previously examined and found to be deficient.

But a moral defense of selective prohibition need not rehearse one of the foregoing rationales for criminalization. Sometimes moral condemnation is reserved for illicit drugs because they are said to be implicated in a more amorphous sense that society is deteriorating. According to this school of thought, the recreational use of illicit drugs is not wrongful because it directly causes some particular problem, but because it is indirectly responsible for a wide variety of social ills. Illicit drug use has been blamed for breakups in marriage, trends in teenage pregnancies, the erosion of civil discourse, a worsening of education, a decline in religious faith, and just about everything else that is said to be wrong with contemporary society. Real evidence linking drug use to these social pathologies is rarely produced. Moreover, alcohol is more strongly implicated in most of these effects. Demographics help to explain the perception that illicit drugs in particular contribute to social decay. Our attitudes about given drugs are shaped by our attitudes about the persons who use them. Illicit drug use is prevalent among adolescents and young adults. Most quit using illicit drugs before they reach middle age. Licit drugs, by contrast, are more likely to be used throughout the entire lifetime. Every generation of adults has accused the next generation of leading society downhill. But the fact that illicit drugs tend to be used most widely by the very group of persons who are always blamed for social deterioration does not express a real cause-and-effect relationship.

A few prohibitionists have risen to the challenge and endeavored to explain why they believe that the recreational use of illicit drugs is immoral, whereas the recreational use of licit drugs is not. James Q. Wilson writes:

> If we believe – as I do – that dependency on certain mindaltering drugs is a moral issue, and that their illegality rests in part on their immorality, then legalizing them undercuts, if it does not eliminate altogether, the moral message. That message is at the root of the distinction we now make between nicotine and cocaine. Both are highly addictive; both have harmful

physical effects. But we treat the two drugs differently, not simply because nicotine is so widely used to be beyond the reach of effective prohibition, but because its use does not destroy the user's essential humanity. Tobacco shortens one's life, cocaine debases it. Nicotine alters one's habits, cocaine alters one's soul.[19]

How are we to understand this attempt to differentiate between the morality of licit and that of illicit drug use? After all, Wilson does not mention the protection of youth, a rise in crime, a decline in health, or a general deterioration in society to support the distinction he draws. Wilson's reference to the "soul" provides the key to an answer. The use of illicit drugs is said to "alter" or "destroy" the soul. On the basis of this allegation, Wilson is prepared to send illicit drug users to prison, while sparing those who use licit drugs such as tobacco and alcohol. How might his allegation be assessed? Millions of living Americans have used cocaine and heroin. If we examine their souls, would we discover them to be altered or destroyed? Would we find the souls of users of licit drugs to be intact?

I cannot really believe that Wilson is intending to make an empirical claim about what doctors and scientists would learn if they studied the souls of illicit drug users. Instead, I suspect he is using *religious* grounds to object to the use of illicit drugs. Contemporary discussions of drug policy rarely mention religion explicitly. I believe this neglect is unfortunate; religion plays an absolutely central role in shaping contemporary drug policy. In Chapter 2, I encouraged readers to begin the debate about drug policy by asking friends and neighbors whether they really believe that people should be punished simply for using illicit drugs. Unfortunately, I cannot guarantee that even those friends and neighbors who generally welcome intellectual exchange will be eager to entertain this question. Frank discussions of drug policy are likely to provoke hostility and anger. Few people seem willing to examine

19 James Q. Wilson, "Against the Legalization of Drugs," in James Inciardi and Karen McElrath, eds., *The American Drug Scene*, 2d ed. (Los Angeles: Roxbury, 1998), pp. 304, 311.

this issue dispassionately. Fair-minded citizens are generally prepared to consider and evaluate competing arguments about the merits or demerits of policies involving such issues as education, health care, and social security. Drug policy, by contrast, tends to evoke a very different kind of response. Although reasonable arguments can be made on both sides, a discussion of this issue will not always be civil or friendly.

Why do controversies about drugs tend to cause people to become so angry and emotional? No single answer accounts for the passion people seem to feel about this issue. To a large extent, however, the inability or unwillingness to engage in a civil and informed debate about illicit drugs reflects the fact that personal opinion on this topic tends to be strongly influenced by religion. Attitudes about drugs and drug policy correlate with age, race, geographical location, political affiliation, and gender. But no demographic variable correlates nearly as strongly with attitudes about illicit drugs as religion. Lifetime abstainers frequently mention religion when asked to explain how they have managed to resist the lure of illicit drugs. Polls indicate that a majority of respondents who identify themselves as having "no religion" believe that marijuana should be "made legal." Protestants, by contrast, oppose legalization by a wide margin. The United States is probably more religious than any Western industrialized democracy; it is no coincidence that the United States has the most punitive drug policy. We should not be surprised that issues closely linked to religion are impossible to resolve by rational argument. In this respect, attitudes about drugs resemble those about abortion, in which religion plays an even more central role. Religious conviction, almost by definition, is the product of faith rather than reason.

Of course, religious faith provides a bad rationale for punishing drug users. Our fundamental question asks for a reason that justifies the criminalization of drug use. Religious faith provides no real answer to this question because it fails to offer *a reason* at all. We live in a secular state in which people should not be punished for behaving in ways that are contrary to the teachings of religion. A justification for punishment must not presuppose that we all share the same religious convictions.

I conclude that we should reject both the major and the minor premise in this syllogism for criminalization. We should be unwilling to allow people to be punished simply because their behavior is immoral. Even more importantly, we have no good reason to believe that the recreational use of illicit drugs *is* immoral. Therefore, this rationale for criminalization fares no better than its predecessors. But one more crucial point remains to be made before we leave this rationale behind. Prohibitionists pretend to occupy the high moral ground in debates about illicit drug use. Unlike their opponents, they profess to stand up against immorality. Those who oppose criminalization are seemingly placed in the uncomfortable and awkward position of condoning behavior that is suspect from a moral point of view.

The moral high ground should *not* be conceded to those who favor prohibition. Disagreement about the immorality of recreational drug use is reasonable. But there can be no disagreement about the immorality of punishing people without excellent reasons to do so. Punishment is the most powerful weapon available to the state, and we must always be vigilant to ensure that it is not inflicted without adequate justification. The central contention of my half of this book is that this weapon is invoked without good reason against recreational drug users. If I am correct, prohibitionists are more clearly guilty of immorality than their opponents. The wrongfulness of recreational drug use, if it exists at all, pales against the immorality of punishing drug users. How much harm to drug users and to society are prohibitionists willing to tolerate in their (mostly futile) efforts to prevent people from taking drugs? I conclude that those who punish drug users perpetrate a far greater immorality than those who merely use drugs.

4   Reasons to Decriminalize

S UPPOSE we agree with my conclusion that the previous reasons are not good enough – not nearly good enough – to
justify prohibition. To my mind, this concession provides all of
the support that decriminalization needs. No one should be punished without excellent reason to do so – a reason grounded in
the desert of the person to be punished. The absence of a good
reason establishes that decriminalization is the just and sensible
position for the state to adopt toward recreational drug users.

Still, the case in favor of decriminalization can be improved.
Although there may be no good reason *to* punish drug users, are
there any good reasons *not* to do so? If the answer is yes – if we
can provide positive reasons in favor of decriminalization – my
conclusion will be bolstered. In this chapter, I will briefly present
the affirmative case for decriminalization. This case contains two
parts. Many critics of drug prohibition have argued at length that
our present policy of punishing drug users is ineffective and counterproductive. These allegations are powerful, and I will discuss
them in the second half of this chapter. But the defense of decriminalization need not rest entirely on the disastrous consequences
of criminalization. I believe there are many reasons to oppose
prohibition, even if our present policy *could* be made to work.
The belief that a war cannot be won without consequences that
are worse than the evil we are combating is not the only reason
to declare a truce. The objective for which we are fighting might
not justify the war in the first place.

The Value of Drug Use

The argument against criminalization presented in Chapter 3 does not presuppose that recreational drug use has any positive benefits. To this point, my position is that the reasons in favor of selective prohibition are not good enough to justify the drastic step of punishing drug users. This position is consistent with the belief that recreational drug use has no value whatever – no more value than acts such as digging holes and filling them up. The argument thus far is incomplete. Suppose I am correct that we lack a good reason to punish drug users. We might still ask, How good a reason do we really need? Since punishment is the worst thing our state can do to us, I have suggested that the justification for punishing anyone – even those who dig holes and fill them up – had better be strong.

But the strength of the reason we require cannot be unrelated to the value of the activity for which punishment is imposed. If drug use has absolutely no value, we need a less weighty reason before we allow it to be criminalized. But if drug use has some value, we should demand a better reason to criminalize it. Moreover, we are more likely to decide that illicit drug use is not morally wrongful if we believe it can produce some beneficial results. Therefore, a full evaluation of the injustice of punishing drug users depends on whether we should attach any value to the use of drugs for recreational purposes. Is there some good that is brought about by recreational drug use? In other words, does recreational drug use have any positive value? In this section, I will address this important question.[1] Ultimately, I will try to describe what I take the value of recreational drug use to be. First, however, I want to indicate why the question itself is peculiar.

In a free society, we typically allow consumers themselves to judge whether the activities in which they engage are worthwhile. If we choose to spend millions of dollars on hula hoops, pet rocks, or the latest fashion craze, it is not the job of government

---

1 A balanced defense of the value of drug use is provided by Jacob Sullum, *Saying Yes: In Defense of Drug Use* (New York: Jeremy P. Tarcher/Putnam, 2003).

(or anyone else) to tell us we may not do so – much less to punish us if we disagree. In the absence of fraud or duress, sane adults should be permitted to find value in whatever they want – unless there are good reasons to prevent them from doing so (a possibility I argued against in Chapter 3). The fact that tens of millions of Americans choose to use illicit drugs each year may be all the evidence of value we should require.

When consumers are granted this freedom, we must be prepared to accept that some will elect to engage in activities that seem strange and unusual to many of us. Individuals often care passionately about pursuits that appear to be trivial and meaningless to others. Any number of examples could be given; I will mention only one. Most of us are acquainted with fanatical sports fans. They follow their favorite team around the country. Every victory fills them with pride and glee; every loss is an occasion for gloom and despair. Notice how difficult it would be for fans to defend that passion if they were called upon to do so. After all, none of their friends or relatives is a member of the team; they do not know any players personally. They have no financial stake in the prosperity of the team. They might admit that they would feel just as devoted to a different team if they had been born in some other city. Yet there is not much in life they care about more deeply than the success of their favorite team.

Fortunately, our fanatical fans need *not* defend their passion. The state does not tell them that their preferred activity is unimportant. Any philosopher who reported that he could find no value in this activity would be told by the fan to mind his own business. We do not demand that those who enjoy such pursuits must explain why they attach so much meaning to them. We allow people the liberty to act according to their own preferences, however odd they may seem to the rest of us. This willingness is the central mark of a free society. Of course, I do not mean to suggest that we have an unlimited freedom to find value in *any* activity. Surely it *is* the business of the state when someone claims to find value in child abuse or murder. These crimes are concerns of the state because a just society protects the rights of persons who are victimized by them.

The sports fan, however, need not harm or violate the rights of anyone.

The difficulty of defending the value of an activity is especially acute when it is purely recreational – pursued for pleasure, euphoria, satisfaction, or some other positive psychological state. If I find a given activity to be enjoyable, I am typically at a loss to explain my reaction to someone who disagrees with me. This is certainly true of taste in foods. Suppose that I love the flavor of anchovies. How can I possibly hope to persuade someone who detests this food to share my preference? Clearly, the whole endeavor is bizarre. Why should we have to defend the value of the fun and enjoyment we experience when we engage in an activity we like? Many moral philosophers have claimed that pleasure is intrinsically valuable. In fact, some have gone so far as to say that pleasure and the absence of pain are the *only* things that are intrinsically valuable. We should not be made to feel shallow and superficial when we admit that our only reason for doing something is that we find it to be pleasant and enjoyable.

Nor should we be apologetic or embarrassed if the particular activity we find to be pleasant and enjoyable involves the use of a *drug*. Invariably, the decision to use illicit drugs for recreational purposes is attributed to peer pressure, boredom, alienation, immaturity, compulsion, ignorance, depression, or some other pathological condition. Even tolerant, liberal abstainers tend to believe that users of illicit drugs need treatment. But empirical support for these preconceptions is dubious; some surveys find that adolescents who have high self-esteem are more likely to use licit drugs than those whose self-confidence is low. In any event, no one proposes comparable pathological explanations about the popularity of *licit* drugs. Punishment or mandatory treatment is never recommended for wine connoisseurs. As is so much else about prohibition, attitudes about *why* people use drugs are extraordinarily selective. In fact, people have exactly the same reasons to use licit and illicit drugs. After all, no known societies – except perhaps that of Eskimos – refrain from using drugs for recreational purposes. Drug use is so pervasive that researchers such as Andrew Weil have speculated that the desire to alter consciousness periodically is an innate, normal drive analogous to hunger or sex.[2]

With these observations in mind, consider the remark of William Bennett about the preferences of illicit drug users. According to Bennett, "A citizen in a drug-induced haze . . . is not what the founding fathers meant by the 'pursuit of happiness.'" It is tempting to respond to Bennett's claim by setting the historical record straight. Drug use – much of it illicit – was hardly unknown among the founding fathers. But the more basic point is not historical. Bennett distorts and misrepresents the wisdom of those who created the political system in which we live. In a free society, the state is no more entitled to devalue the activity of the drug user than that of the fanatical sports fan.

Why is the value of recreational drug use so difficult to comprehend and acknowledge? We should recognize a widespread psychological tendency to *de*value activities that we ourselves do not like. People who love to ski can appreciate the exhilaration of those who share their passion. Others may be baffled to understand why anyone would bother to make the effort. This psychological tendency is pervasive in our attitudes about drugs – both licit and illicit. If we loathe the smell of cigars, we cannot fathom how anyone could possibly enjoy them. In our more thoughtful moments, however, we realize that tastes differ, and that our own preferences give us no reason to limit the freedom of those who disagree with us.

To this point, I have called attention to the peculiarity of demanding that drug users defend their preference. We do not impose comparable requirements on those who watch soap operas or patronize amusement parks. But we cannot expect to satisfy those who make this demand by telling them to mind their own business. We all know that recreation is valuable, despite the curious and indefensible exception that is made when illicit drugs provide the source of the positive psychological state we seek. If we agree, we must be willing to allow people to undertake some risks when engaged in recreational activities. We sympathize with

2 Andrew Weil, *The Natural Mind*, 2d ed. (Boston: Houghton Mifflin, 1986).

those who use dangerous drugs to treat a medical condition – a condition that qualifies as a disease or illness. Evidently, however, no hazard is worth risking when that same drug is used simply to gain pleasure or euphoria.

Our refusal to tolerate any level of risk when drug use is recreational is very hard to defend. After all, no drug is without risks and side effects. According to 1998 estimates, prescription drugs cause about 100,000 fatalities each year in the United States – even when these drugs are used exactly as prescribed.[3] This figure far exceeds the most pessimistic estimates of deaths caused by illicit drugs. Why do we tolerate these staggering levels of risk? The answer can only be the value we attach to health. When a drug used for recreational purposes gives rise to relatively minor risks – as with the dehydration associated with ecstasy – the state responds by increasing the severity of criminal penalties. Why do we not allow these lesser risks? Again, the answer can only be the lack of value we attach to recreation. The key to understanding our present drug policy, then, is to realize that the use of recreational drugs is regarded as having so little value that it fails to justify even the smallest risks. This is why our drug policy places medical and recreational use in entirely different categories.

Notice that we allow people to take enormous risks when they engage in recreational activities that do *not* involve the use of drugs. Consider the risks of skydiving, skiing, or scuba diving. These recreational activities are dangerous – more dangerous than any widely used illicit drug. Still, we do not require individuals to have a very good reason, such as the need to cure a disease or illness, before we allow these risks to be taken. Why not? The answer is that we attach value to these activities. More precisely, we are willing to allow people to decide for themselves whether they value these activities. Even when we do not fathom why anyone would jump out of an airplane with a parachute simply for the thrill, we defer to the judgments of those who disagree with us about whether such activities are worth the danger. Sometimes

3 See Jason Latrou et al., "Incidence of Adverse Drug Reactions in Hospitalized Patients," 279 *Journal of the American Medical Association* 1200 (1998).

we even admire people who undertake enormous risks in recreational activities such as mountain climbing. We write books and make movies about their courage. Why, then, are medical reasons required before we allow people to undertake the lesser risks inherent in drug use? Why do we punish people for the risks they take by using illicit drugs recreationally, when virtually no other dangerous recreational activity is punished? I have no good answers to these important questions, which lie at the heart of our drug policy.

Recreational objectives turn out to be important even in populations with a medical need for illicit drugs. Results from the medical marijuana research project at the San Mateo Medical Center confirm this claim.[4] The first clinical trials of HIV patients, which ended in 2003, surprised many psychologists. The study indicated that more HIV patients smoked marijuana for mental than for physical reasons. Researchers expected that patients would smoke marijuana to alleviate nausea or pain or to increase appetite. But 57 percent said they smoked simply to relieve anxiety or depression, and only 28 percent indicated that they smoked to reduce pain. Use that seemingly qualifies as recreational is dominant even among populations who suffer from a serious disease.

Can we say more about the value of drug use? Many opponents of prohibition have gone to great lengths to describe the benefits of drug use in terms that others can comprehend. The most familiar strategy is to show how the use of drugs may help to promote some objective that is universally acknowledged to be valuable. Some have contended that drug use opens doors to spiritual enlightenment. Others have emphasized the advantages of drugs in fostering literary and artistic creativity. Still others have stressed the importance of controlling one's own state of consciousness.

This latter claim is especially plausible. In 2003, the United States Supreme Court upheld the right to refuse unwanted psychotropic medication in its landmark decision of *Sell v. United States*, ruling in favor of a dentist charged with Medicaid fraud who was found incompetent to stand trial because of paranoid

4 See http://www.onlinepot.org/medicalaidwave.htm.

delusions. Dr. Sell succeeded in resisting state efforts to force him to take antipsychotic drugs. The Court held that administration of involuntary medication solely to make individuals competent to stand trial would be appropriate only in very rare circumstances. If the state cannot require persons with paranoid delusions to take drugs to become normal, why it can forbid psychologically healthy adults to use drugs to alter their own consciousness is unclear. By ruling in favor of Dr. Sell, the Court apparently vindicated the fundamental right of every American to control his or her own thought processes.

In what follows, however, I will not explore these kinds of benefits in any detail; I make no grandiose claims about the significance of illicit drugs or the right to control one's own state of consciousness. My focus is solely on the value of *recreational* drug use. To inquire more deeply into the nature of this value, we need to understand why so many people choose to use drugs – licit or illicit – for recreational purposes. Surprisingly little research on this topic exists. Of course, no single explanation can be given. The best explanation, however, is *mood control*. We often say that moods are beyond our control and "come over us," but these statements are exaggerations. In fact, we have many devices to help us to alter our moods. Drugs play a central role in this process. Consider the particular circumstances in which different licit drugs are used. Caffeine is consumed mostly in the morning, when people are drowsy and lethargic. Alcohol is used mostly in the evening, when people want to unwind and relax. Without these recreational drugs, many would be condemned to remain sleepy in the morning, and tense in the evening. These drugs allow us to change our moods in desired ways at given times and places. By this means, users of licit drugs exercise more control over their life and thereby increase their enjoyment.[5]

This explanation is equally applicable to illicit drugs. Users take them in order to alter their mood in desired directions. Interviews

5 For a description of how adolescents use drugs to regulate moods, see Howard Parker, Judith Aldridge, and Fiona Measham, *Illegal Leisure: The Normalization of Adolescent Recreational Drug Use* (London: Routledge, 1998).

with recreational users of illicit drugs consistently indicate that people choose which drugs to take, and when to take them, in order to feel the way they believe is appropriate for the situation. Marijuana is used to relax; LSD is taken to have fun; amphetamines and ecstasy are taken to become energetic. This explanation for why people take drugs for recreational purposes may fly in the face of conventional wisdom. Many abstainers say they do not take drugs because they do not want to lose control. Presumably, they are thinking about debilitating dosages of recreational drugs when they make this criticism. In moderate amounts, however, I have suggested that drug use actually *increases* control. Admittedly, users do not always *succeed* in achieving the mood they desire. But no recreational activity is uniformly rewarding.

If I am correct, recreational drug use has positive value. I have tried not to exaggerate the extent of this value. I have not relied on grand claims that portray drugs as the key to personal fulfillment or spiritual enlightenment. Most of the value of recreational drug use consists in simple fun and euphoria – goods that should require no elaborate defense. More specifically, the ability to alter mood in desired ways at given times and places can increase control over life and add to its enjoyment. Our assessment of the injustice of prohibition is incomplete unless we take the value of illicit drug use into account. When this value is added to the inquiry, the injustice of punishing recreational users of illicit drugs becomes even more apparent.

Drug Prohibition as Counterproductive

The injustice of criminalization provides the best reason to abandon punitive policies that fill our jails and prisons with illicit drug users. But some readers may still be unmoved – even if they accept my arguments thus far. The considerations I have described may seem too abstract and distant from our personal experience to change our mind. If our own friends or family members are unlikely to face punishment, we may not care about the injustice done to others. After all, the drugs that most of *us* consume are not prohibited. Surely criminalization has achieved some benefits, even though the rationales in its favor are less persuasive than we would like. And what harm does prohibition really bring about? Of course, it harms the victims of injustice, but how does that affect the rest of us? Unfortunately, the world is full of injustice. Why should we be concerned about *this* injustice in particular?

Many other commentators have answered this question. Although justice provides the *best* reason to oppose criminalization, it does not provide the *only* reason. Drug prohibition has caused a great deal of harm – harm that affects us all, whether or not we ever face punishment for using an illicit drug. Our drug policy harms us all because it is *counterproductive*. In the remainder of this chapter, I will describe several bad consequences that are caused by the fact that illicit drug users are punished. Criminalization would have to accomplish enormous benefits in order to justify a policy that produces all of the harms I will describe. I believe that our punitive policies do *not* accomplish enough benefits to outweigh these harms. On this ground alone, decriminalization represents a preferable component of a drug policy.

In this section I list seven respects in which our policy of punishing illicit drug users is counterproductive. In other words, I describe seven distinct bad consequences of prohibition. This list is far from exhaustive; criminalization is counterproductive in many ways I do not mention. The discussions that follow are cursory and incomplete; books could be written about each of these harmful consequences of prohibition.[6] In fact, books *have* been written about each of these topics. Since other critics of criminalization have examined these problems in impressive detail, and since my own focus is on the *injustice* of prohibition, my discussion of these consequences is brief.

In the first place, prohibition has always been aimed – or selectively enforced – against minorities. Contemporary statistics are shocking. Although whites and blacks are roughly comparable

---

6 The classic source is the brief article by Ethan Nadelmann, "Drug Prohibition in the United States: Costs, Consequences, and Alternatives," 245 *Science* 939 (1989).

in their rates of illicit drug use, blacks are arrested, prosecuted, and punished for drug offenses far more frequently and harshly than whites. About 10 million whites and 2 million blacks are current users of illicit drugs. Five times more whites than blacks use marijuana, and about four times more whites than blacks use cocaine. Whites outnumber blacks even in the case of crack, the illicit drug most commonly associated with minorities. In fact, the majority of users of *any* illicit drug are white. But even though white drug users outnumber blacks by a 5 to 1 margin, blacks constitute 62.7 percent and whites 36.7 percent of all drug offenders admitted to state prisons. Most commentators agree that these facts prove our drug policy is racially biased. Selective prohibition would have vanished long ago if whites had been sent to prison for drug offenses at the same rate as blacks.

In addition, drug prohibition is destructive to public health. Since the vast majority of illicit drugs taken for recreational purposes are purchased on the street from unlicensed sellers, consumers can have no confidence about what they are buying. Even sellers rarely know the exact content of the substances they distribute. Street drugs may contain deadly impurities, and unknown potencies can contribute to deaths from overdose. Admittedly, major progress in making drugs less dangerous would require legalization, extending decriminalization beyond use to include production and sale. Enormous gains could result if state oversight of illicit drugs were comparable to the Food and Drug Administration's supervision of foods and licit drugs. We take for granted that the substances we consume contain only those ingredients that are listed on the labels. But illicit drugs are not subject to any quality controls.

We have no idea how safe illicit drug use could be made to be if the best minds in the pharmaceutical industry were focused on this objective. Consider the hazards of ecstasy, which derive almost exclusively from an increase in body temperature that leads to organ failure. In 2003, researchers discovered that mice who lacked a specific protein were able to stay cool after being injected with ecstasy. This discovery may lead us to find a way to deactivate the protein and prevent the body from overheating.

But this safeguard may never be incorporated into the ecstasy that users actually consume as long as production and sale remain illegal.

Next, consider the pernicious role that drugs continue to play in our foreign policy. The war on drugs has come to resemble the cold war, when governments with dismal records on human rights were befriended solely because of their opposition to communism. Today, corrupt regimes are supported for no reason other than their alleged willingness to join the fight against drugs. To cite only one of many possible examples, the United States sent millions of dollars to help the Taliban eradicate heroin in Afghanistan. We will never know how much of this aid was diverted to finance acts of terrorism against our people.

Truth is among the foremost casualties of our misguided drug policy. The demonization of illicit drugs is so pervasive that frank and honest discourse is all but impossible. Policies are implemented and perpetuated not because they are believed to be effective, but because our leaders are worried about the reactions of voters if they are discontinued. Politicians and parents alike squirm to explain their history of illicit drug use as a "youthful indiscretion." More frequently, they simply lie. Politics and dishonesty, not science and candor, continue to fuel our drug policy.

Prohibition has eroded precious civil liberties in which Americans take pride. Many legal theorists speak openly of the "drug exception" to the Bill of Rights. Since illicit drugs are easy to conceal and involve consensual transactions that typically occur behind closed doors, police have been forced to resort to unusual and questionable tactics to enforce criminalization. Among other abuses, drug prohibitions have given rise to "racial profiling" by law enforcement. These tactics should not surprise us. When laws are enacted that make criminals of millions of Americans, it is naïve to expect them to be enforced in a fair and evenhanded way. We must be critical of policies that can only be implemented by the sacrifice of our civil liberties.

There may be no greater threat to the rule of law than corruption and abuse of authority among government officials. Prohibition and the huge amounts of money in the illicit drug trade create irresistible temptations for law-enforcement agents to place themselves above the law. The United Nations Drug Control Program noted the inevitable risk of police corruption wherever there is a well-organized, illicit drug industry. This danger is especially grave in drug-producing countries. But no one should underestimate the extent of corruption in the United States itself.

The seventh and final counterproductive effect of selective prohibition I will mention is the easiest to understand. Our punitive drug policies cost exorbitant amounts of money. State and federal governments now spend close to $40 billion each year combating illegal drugs. Most of this money has been wasted.[7] If we stopped punishing drug users, taxpayers would reap enormous savings. Modest improvements in our drug policy may finally result from the urgent need of governments to reduce their massive budget deficits.

I have provided a very brief sketch of seven respects in which our punitive drug policy is counterproductive and detrimental to us all – drug users and nonusers alike. Perhaps I have overlooked a particular effect that is more worrisome than those I have discussed. Or we might quibble about whether I have exaggerated or distorted the evidence in one example or another. In combination, however, these allegations provide a powerful indictment of prohibition. No reasonable person can dismiss all of these problems as insignificant and unimportant. Those who support the punishment of illicit drug users may respond by pointing out that any war – including the war on drugs – will exact a terrible price. That price, however, must be worth paying. No policy should be perpetuated unless its objective is sufficiently important to justify the collateral damage we know has occurred and have every reason to believe will continue to occur. What *is* that important objective? I have argued that there is no good answer to this fundamental question – no adequate justification for punishing people simply for using (some) drugs for recreational purposes. But the grave injustice to drug users is hardly the only reason to oppose prohibition.

---

7 For an economist's perspective, see Jeffrey A. Miron, *Drug War Crimes: The Consequences of Prohibition* (Oakland, CA: The Independent Institute, 2004).

5 Drug Legalization: Production and Sale

S UPPOSE I am correct that some or even all of the drugs presently criminalized for recreational purposes should be decriminalized. This conclusion, although defensible on grounds of justice, only begins to describe a comprehensive drug policy. A complete account must take a position on the thorny issue of *production* and *sale* of decriminalized drugs. A given drug is *legalized* when its production and sale are not criminal offenses. *Should* newly decriminalized drugs be legalized? This is the issue I propose to address in this final chapter. My discussion will only scratch the surface of this complex topic.

The first point to recall is that drug decriminalization and legalization are separate issues. Decriminalization, as I have defined it, has no direct implications for production or sale. It is entirely consistent with punishing producers and/or sellers of newly decriminalized drugs. Many official government reports – such as that of the Shafer Commission – have made this very recommendation, at least for marijuana.[1] Anyone who believes that this combination of policies is incoherent should be reminded of our nation's history. From 1920 to 1933 – the era known simply as *prohibition* – the sale (or production for sale) of alcohol was a federal offense. But the *use* of alcohol was not a crime. Of course, few historians believe this combination of policies worked well. Some go so far as to describe it as a disaster. Still, alcohol prohibition was

---

1 The complete text of the Shafer Commission Report is available at http://www.druglibrary.org/schaffer/Library/stusies/nc/ncmenu.htm.

a reality. Thus there is no *inconsistency* in believing that the use of a substance should *not* be a crime, even though the production and sale of that substance *should* be.

If drug decriminalization would allow production and sale to be prohibited, what benefits would it accomplish? Many of the objectives that reformers seek – an elimination of the black market, greater tax revenues, and the like – would not be achieved if we continued to punish those who produce and sell illicit drugs. Anyone who is attracted to drug law reform for economic reasons is almost certain to want to remove criminal penalties for production and sale as well as for use. But economic gain is not the best reason to oppose prohibition. Our criminal laws must be just. From this perspective, decriminalization as I have characterized it would represent enormous progress. Since millions of Americans have been arrested, and hundreds of thousands have been jailed or imprisoned merely for using an illicit drug – unjustly, as I have argued – decriminalization would dramatically improve our system of criminal law. This gain in justice would be achieved even if we continued to punish drug producers and sellers and thereby failed to reap the economic rewards of legalization.

Still, I propose to examine what can be said on behalf of legalization. No simple account will suffice. Some commentators accept the slogan "Whatever is legal to use *must* be legal to produce and sell." I think this slogan is simplistic; very different arguments apply to the two issues. Admittedly, some of the same principles are at stake. Punishment must be deserved and cannot be justified in the absence of compelling reasons – regardless of whether it is imposed on users, producers, or sellers. In Chapter 3, I indicated that no good argument has been given in favor of punishing drug users. But there *may* be compelling reasons to punish producers and/or sellers of drugs. We will not know until these arguments are placed on the table. In any event, this issue must be examined on its own merits, without supposing it has been resolved by deciding that no good argument has been given to criminalize use.

To begin, we must distinguish two very different issues. The first pertains to production for personal use. Some illicit drugs are produced by the same individuals who consume them. I assume that anyone who endorses decriminalization will allow persons to produce whatever drugs they use. Moreover, punishment should not be inflicted on those who freely exchange the drugs they produce for consumption by their friends and families. If I am correct, the difficult issue does not involve personal production and sale, but *commercial* transactions. That is, the difficult issue of legalization is about production and sale *for profit*. Once the controversy about legalization is clarified in this way, seeing that different principles are at stake from those that pertain to decriminalization is easy. These differences emerge in many other contexts – most notably, in our policy about freedom of speech. Although the right to speak has long been regarded as fundamental to a free society, the liberty to profit from speech is much less important. Thus commercial advertising is properly regulated in the public interest. Recreational drug use and freedom of speech are similar in this respect. In Chapter 4, I suggested that recreational drug use might be valuable. Drug use is as valuable as many other recreational activities and plays an especially important role in altering mood. Obviously, these benefits are not present in commercial production or sale. No one manufactures or sells drugs for sheer enjoyment or mood elevation. I do not mean to denigrate the profit motive; I simply point out that its value is wholly unlike that which applies to recreational drug use.[2]

Public opinion is steadily moving toward a system in which marijuana, at least, is not only decriminalized, but also legalized. In a nationwide poll conducted in 2003, 41 percent of Americans agreed that "the government should treat marijuana more or less the same way it treats alcohol: it should regulate it, control it, tax it and only make it illegal for children." Still, I have argued that these issues should not be resolved by public opinion polls. What criterion, then, *should* be applied to decide whether to accept or reject various legalization schemes? I am inclined to think that a harm-reduction framework should be applied

---

2 Libertarians tend to challenge the idea that personal drug use and commercial transactions implicate different interests. See, for example, Thomas Szasz, *Our Right to Drugs: The Case for a Free Market* (New York: Praeger, 1992).

to assess questions about commercialization – that is, to issues about legalization. I have argued that our punitive policies toward drug users cannot be justified as a means to protect adolescents, safeguard health, or prevent crime. But the combination of policies imposed on sellers or producers of drugs might be tailored to help achieve these objectives. Consider some unresolved issues. Should drugs be sold in "state stores" run by the government? Or should they be sold by the private sector? Would advertising or other forms of promotion be allowed? Which kinds? These (and myriad other) questions are difficult and important. It is hard to see why one answer is preferable to another on grounds of justice. In all probability, the solution requires us to identify the alternative that minimizes harm.

The main worry about legalization – expressed forcefully by de Marneffe in the context of heroin – is its impact on rates of drug use and abuse. Without a detailed model to evaluate, predictions are tenuous. We know from our experience with tobacco and alcohol that nonusers are less likely to begin to use drugs if they are expensive. Thus it is especially important to comment on how legalization would affect the monetary cost of decriminalized drugs. Price would depend mainly on two variables. First, legalization would suddenly make drugs subject to taxation. States that levy sizable taxes on alcohol and tobacco would certainly impose high taxes on illicit drugs as well. The amount of this tax is hard to estimate and would differ from place to place. States would be expected to impose a tax that is sufficiently high to retard consumption. Still, taxes could not be too high. Many of the advantages of legalization would not be attained if high taxes caused the reappearance of a black market. I leave to economists the arduous task of calculating the optimal rate of taxation. Whatever the exact figure, we can be sure that taxes would add significantly to the cost of newly legalized drugs.

The second factor affecting the price of legalized drugs is even more difficult to estimate. If illicit drugs are anywhere near as dangerous as many people believe, some mechanism must be created to compensate victims for the harms they suffer when drugs are abused. These harms are of two kinds. First, drug users might harm themselves. As for smokers of tobacco, users of illicit drugs might make more frequent visits to doctors and hospitals. Second, drug users might harm others. As for drinkers of alcohol, users of illicit drugs might cause more accidents. One way to compensate victims for each of these kinds of harms is to allow lawsuits against producers and sellers of illicit drugs. We have been hesitant to allow such lawsuits in the cases of tobacco and alcohol; powerful lobbies have fought against them for years. But we need not be so reluctant when we establish a new system of production and sale for legalized drugs. Commercial entities could be made to pay for the costs of the various harms that their customers cause to themselves and to others. Producers and sellers would be able to remain in business only by passing on these costs to buyers in the form of higher prices. How much of an increase would be needed to compensate all of the victims for the harms they suffer when newly legalized drugs are used?

Of course, we cannot begin to answer this question unless we know how dangerous illicit drugs really are. I have claimed that the dangers of illicit drugs tend to be exaggerated. Even if I am mistaken about the dangers of illicit drugs today, we can be confident that drugs would become far less dangerous after production and sale were made lawful. After legalization, suppliers would have enormous incentives to make their drugs as safe as possible in order to limit the amount of money they would be required to pay when harm was caused by the use of their products. If a given drug is very dangerous, we might even find that no company is able to make a profit by selling it, and the drug would disappear from the lawful market. We simply do not know how dangerous legalized drugs will turn out to be; to this point, producers have had no motivation to improve the safety of their products. But financial incentives are bound to make illicit drugs less hazardous.

As a result of these two factors, we have almost no basis for estimating how the monetary price of legalized drugs would differ from their price in the black market. We do not know how much states will decide to tax the sale of drugs. In addition, we do not know how much sellers will have to charge in order to survive when lawsuits are brought against them. If this latter figure were high, drugs would be expensive, and concerns about cheap drugs would be put to rest. If this figure were low, the price of drugs would decrease. But if the amount sellers had to charge as a result of these lawsuits were low, that would mean that drugs turned out to be less dangerous than we feared. If drugs are not as dangerous as we feared, we will come to wonder why we were so worried about making them more affordable in the first place. The general point is clear. Those who tend to trust the pricing mechanisms of the market should not assume that these mechanisms will fail in the case of legalized drugs. At the very least, we should not assume that dangerous drugs would suddenly become cheap after they were legalized.

Still, monetary price is not the only variable that will affect rates of drug use. When production and sale are no longer punished, almost all commentators anticipate a substantial increase in use. How great an increase should we expect? No one should pretend to know. My own conjecture is that the criminal law has less impact on rates of drug use than several nonlegal factors, so a change in our statutes will be less significant than many defenders of the status quo predict. Cultural norms about whether drugs are cool or foolish are more important factors. It is impossible to anticipate how social attitudes about drug use will vary after we become accustomed to legalization. Predictions about these attitudes are as tenuous as those about trends in music or fashion.

In any event, greater amounts of use need not cause greater amounts of social harm. Many harm-reduction initiatives other than taxation are compatible with legalization. I see no injustice in rules that regulate consumption in the public interest, as long as they do not unreasonably burden use. These include educational programs, bans on advertising, age restrictions, limitations on time and place of sale and use, specifications of the kinds of activities that may be combined with sale and use, regulations of labeling, and restrictions on quantity and purity. We are accustomed to time, place, and manner restrictions in the exercise of our fundamental right of speech, and many of these same restrictions could be adopted here without fear of injustice. Some clues about the effectiveness of these mechanisms in reducing harm can be found in our experience with licit substances such as alcohol and tobacco. Here, the record is decidedly mixed. Rates of consumption of these products have declined substantially in the past two decades, without the need to resort to criminal penalties for use. At the same time, the number of alcohol abusers has remained fairly constant. Again, however, we should be able to improve on our policies of distributing these licit substances, since we need not compromise with powerful lobbies that profit from maintaining the status quo.

Concerns about legalization typically assume that the drugs of tomorrow will resemble the drugs of today. This assumption seems extraordinarily naïve. The development of new and different substances makes these worries enormously speculative. Many illicit drugs – heroin, ecstasy, and LSD, for example – were originally created by pharmaceutical companies. Legalization may lead these companies to change their priorities in research and development. To date, these companies have not expended their talent or ingenuity to create better and safer recreational drugs. If more enjoyable and less dangerous drugs could be perfected, consumption might boom. But the development of better and safer drugs would make the increase in consumption less of a social problem.

Whether or not new drugs appear on the market and existing drugs vanish, no one can predict how users will substitute newly legalized drugs for existing licit drugs. After legalization, consumers will have lawful alternatives that we generally take for granted in virtually every other context. Users will not have to worry about punishment when attempting to learn which kinds of drugs they prefer. Over time, one would expect that people would gravitate toward those drugs that can be integrated into their lifestyle most easily. Presumably, this tendency accounts for why marijuana is the most widely used illicit drug in the United States today. Marijuana is correctly perceived to be less dangerous, and more easily assimilated into daily activities, than other illicit substances.

If legalization would facilitate substitution among drugs, we have a ready reply to one answer that drug prohibitionists often give when challenged to defend different policies toward licit and illicit drugs. This challenge is familiar: Why is it fair to punish users of marijuana and cocaine, while exempting users of alcohol and tobacco? Many attempts to answer this question have been made; none is persuasive.[3] Here, however, I want to examine *one* particular answer that is given frequently. Prohibitionists typically concede – as they must – that alcohol and tobacco cause tremendous social harm. Why, they ask, should we compound this problem by decriminalizing other drugs that are socially harmful as well?[4] As far as I can see, however, this response evades rather than meets the challenge. It does not even attempt to identify a relevant dissimilarity between those drugs we should allow and those drugs we should prohibit. More importantly for present purposes, this reply seemingly assumes that the legalization of illicit drugs will simply add to the total amount of harm already caused by licit drugs such as alcohol and tobacco. In other words, the consumption of these licit drugs would be unchanged, so any growth in the consumption of illicit drugs caused by legalization would increase the total amount of harm caused by both kinds of drugs combined. But this assumption is dubious. Legalization will allow consumers a much wider choice in the drugs they can take. There is no reason to believe that all (or even most) persons who otherwise would drink alcohol and smoke tobacco would continue to do so if other options became legally available. Many users of these drugs would be expected to switch, and to curtail or even abandon their use of licit drugs altogether. As we know, alcohol and tobacco (along with caffeine) are the drugs most widely used for recreational purposes today. But we should not assume that these drugs would continue to occupy their dominant market position after legalization. We simply do not know whether and to what extent users would substitute newly legalized drugs

---

3 For a nice historical explanation (rather than a defense), see David T. Courtwright, *Forces of Habit: Drugs and the Making of the Modern World* (Cambridge, MA: Harvard University Press, 2001).

4 This defense of the differential treatment of licit and illicit drugs is defended by George Sher, "On the Decriminalization of Drugs," 22 *Criminal Justice Ethics* 30 (winter/spring 2003).

for those licit drugs they now tend to choose. If a great deal of substitution took place, the enormous social harm presently caused by tobacco and alcohol might decline considerably. The total amount of harm caused by both categories of drugs might actually decrease.

In devising a better drug policy we have much to learn from our European neighbors, many of whom are more willing to implement harm-reduction initiatives. We should carefully monitor the approaches of foreign countries to decide what policies are most successful. The Netherlands is famous (or infamous) for tolerating the consumption of marijuana and hashish in licensed coffee shops. Since the Dutch initiated the de facto legalization of marijuana in 1976, we have ample evidence about how their novel experiment has worked. Overall, consumption rates in the Netherlands are probably lower than those in the United States. Recent data indicate that only 21 percent of Dutch citizens aged 12 to 18 have ever tried marijuana, compared to 38 percent of Americans that age.[5] Nor are they more inclined to use cocaine and heroin than their American counterparts. Although there are innumerable differences between Dutch culture and that of the United States, these data are surely better than pure speculation in predicting the effects of legalization. It is hard to believe that this system for distributing drugs is worse than our own underground market. Still, we have few real experiments from which to draw when attempting to create our own legalization regime.

Among the more intriguing possibilities in a scheme of legalization is the proposal to license drug users. Drugs would be sold only to buyers who were licensed. As I indicated in Chapter 1, it is unclear whether such a system should be described as legalization. Much depends on how stringently or leniently licenses are conferred or withdrawn. As far as I can tell, the only serious objection to such a system is its practical feasibility. But before such proposals are dismissed as wholly unrealistic, we need to remind

---

5 See Robert J. MacCoun and Peter Router, *Drug War Heresies: Learning from Other Vices, Times, and Places* (Cambridge: Cambridge University Press, 2001), pp. 252–6.

ourselves how ineffective our present system is in minimizing the harms of drug use. We can readily admit that a new idea is problematic without conceding that it is inferior to the status quo.

Finally, the regime of legalized drugs is hard to describe because it need not be monolithic. No one should be embarrassed by an inability to specify all of the details of an optimal drug policy. It is premature to specify a single blueprint for legalization – for how newly decriminalized drugs should be bought and sold. We will need a great deal of ingenuity and trial and error before we decide what works best. Different states and municipalities should be encouraged to adopt different approaches so that we can base our policies on actual results rather than on speculation and conjecture. Imagine 50 different rates of taxation, 50 different rules for compensating victims of harms caused by drug use, 50 different sets of regulations governing production and sale, and thousands of different sets of rules and incentives created by corporations, schools, and insurance companies. Some but not all of these experiments will be incompatible with justice. Until they are conducted, we should not be so naive as to make confident predictions about how harm can best be minimized in a world of drug legalization. What *is* naive, however, is the smug assurance that our existing system, with its heavy reliance on punishment, produces the least overall harm to society.

Despite the considerable uncertainties that surround legalization, there is *one* prediction of which we *can* be confident. After the legal changes I have proposed here, individuals who use illicit drugs would not face arrest and prosecution. The life of drug users would not be devastated by our criminal justice system.[6] Punishment, we must always be reminded, is the worst thing our state can do to us. The single forecast we can safely make about decriminalization and legalization is that they will dramatically improve the lives of the hundreds of thousands of Americans who otherwise would be arrested and punished for the crime of using drugs for recreational purposes.

---

6 For a description of the consequences of the drug war on individuals, see Mikki Norris, Chris Conrad, and Virginia Resner, *Shattered Lives: Portraits from America's Drug War* (El Cerrito, CA: Creative Xpressions, 2000).

II Against Drug Legalization

Peter de Marneffe

6 An Argument for Drug Prohibition

The General Argument

There is only one good reason for drug prohibition, which is that some of us will be worse off if drugs are legalized. Why would any of us be worse off? With drug legalization there will be more drug abuse, and drug abuse is bad for people.

By "drug abuse" I mean use that (a) harms others or oneself or (b) creates a risk of harm that is great enough either to constitute a wrong to others or to be imprudent. Within the range of harms I mean to include the loss of valuable opportunities and resources as well as damage to a person's physical or psychological health, functioning, or well-being.

Since drug prohibition itself makes drug use harmful in a number of ways – by creating significant risks of criminal liability, for example – it is necessary to distinguish legally created harms from what I will call *independent harms*, which are those that drug use would produce even if drugs were legal. Drug prohibition can be justified only as reducing independent harms since legally created harms would be eliminated by legalization. What independent harms, then, does drug prohibition reduce? This depends on the drug in question, but grouping all currently illegal drugs together we can say that drug prohibition now reduces risks of premature death, accidental bodily injury, violence, vandalism, marital instability, child neglect, and failure at important educational and occupational tasks. This is the argument for drug prohibition, and so against drug legalization.

By *drug legalization* I mean a policy under which there are no criminal penalties for the *manufacture* and *sale* of drugs (to adults). If drugs were legalized, the law would therefore treat drugs such as heroin and cocaine in roughly the same way that it now treats alcohol and cigarettes. Drug legalization in this sense is different from "drug decriminalization," which is the removal of criminal penalties for the *use* of drugs and for the possession of small quantities. In supporting drug *prohibition* here, I oppose drug *legalization*, but not necessarily drug *decriminalization*.

Drug prohibition is justified, in my view, as reducing the independent harms of drug abuse. But it is commonly objected that drug laws "don't work." Does this mean that drug laws do not *eradicate* drug abuse? If so, it is no argument for drug legalization. In this sense laws against murder and theft do not work either, but this does not mean that we should abolish them. The question in evaluating drug prohibition, as in evaluating any coercive policy, is whether it reduces harm to individuals *enough* to justify the burdens imposed on individuals by its system of penalties. We think this is true of laws against murder and theft. So we think they are justified. If this were likewise true of drug prohibition, this policy would likewise be justified.

Does the objection that drug laws do not work mean, then, that they do absolutely *nothing* to reduce drug abuse? If so, this is hard to believe. The main reason people use drugs is that they are enjoyable. If an activity is enjoyable, we can safely predict that more people will engage in it and that individuals will engage in it more often as it becomes easier and less expensive to do. If drugs are legal, they will be easier to acquire because they will be sold at local stores. They will be less expensive because they will be more plentiful and their price will no longer reflect the risks of selling an illegal product: the risks of violence, incarceration, confiscation of property, and so on. Drugs will be safer because they will be sold in standard dosages. Furthermore, the psychological cost of having to deal with unsavory characters in unsafe parts of town in order to buy drugs will be eliminated, as well as the stigma involved in buying an illegal product.

Admittedly it does not follow logically from the premise that drug *use* will increase with legalization that drug *abuse* will also increase. It is *possible* that everyone who is disposed to abuse drugs already uses them illegally and abuses them as much as he or she would if they were legal. Since, however, drug legalization would make it easier to use drugs, it would also make it easier to abuse them. If we assume, then, that a person is more likely to do something she or he is tempted to do the easier and less costly it is, we may reasonably conclude that a person is also more likely to abuse drugs if they are legal. To this we may add that if the manufacture and sale of drugs are legal, drug manufacturers will market them in the same way that alcohol and cigarettes are now marketed. Assuming, then, that such marketing results in people's drinking and smoking more than they otherwise would, we can predict that similar advertising of currently illegal drugs would result in people's using drugs more than they otherwise would, and so in this way also to an increase in drug abuse.

What any honest defender of drug prohibition must still concede is that the mere fact that drug prohibition works to *some* degree is not enough to justify it. It must work *well enough* to justify the burdens it imposes on people. That is, it must decrease the independent harms of drug abuse *enough* to justify the legally created harms it creates. In what follows I will assume that drug prohibition functions to reduce these independent harms *substantially*. I make this assumption because it is what I believe, but I concede that it cannot be proved. I believe that no one is justified in feeling certain *one way or the other* about the degree to which drug prohibition reduces the independent harms of drug abuse. What I aim to do, then, is to offer a philosophical defense of drug prohibition that is consistent with what we know for sure about drug use; that is based on plausible assumptions about human nature; and that represents a morally defensible balancing of the interests of individuals on certain empirical assumptions.

Heroin

Different drugs have different effects. Some, although they may be subject to abuse, are not nearly so harmful as others. So we must always evaluate the policy of prohibition drug by drug. For this reason I begin my defense of drug prohibition by stating an argument for heroin prohibition. I start here because I believe it is easier to make a persuasive case for prohibiting heroin than for prohibiting any other drug, with the possible exception of alcohol. If I am right about this, and the case for heroin prohibition fails, then this is a powerful argument for drug legalization in general. If, on the other hand, the case for heroin prohibition succeeds, then this will provide a good vantage point from which to consider whether good arguments might also be made for prohibiting other drugs.

Heroin has two properties that make it the appropriate object of special concern. One of these is that heroin offers a unique and very intense form of pleasure.[1] This is especially true when heroin is injected, but smoking heroin, which has become more common as purer forms of heroin have become available on the black market, also produces intense pleasure. Not everyone who tries heroin enjoys it, but a high proportion of those who try it say they do.[2] Moreover, heroin users commonly say that heroin is far more pleasurable than anything else they have experienced and sometimes describe an almost religious devotion to it.[3] Because such a high proportion of those who try it enjoy it, and because it is so much more pleasurable to many of them than anything else they might do, we can safely predict an increase in heroin use, and so in heroin abuse, if heroin is legalized.

Why would this be a bad thing? The other important property of heroin is that, as a particularly strong form of opium, it has the effect on some people of sharply depressing their motivation to achieve worthwhile goals and to meet their responsibilities and commitments to others, to go to school or go to work, for example, or to take care of their children. If heroin depresses motivation in this way, then an increase in heroin abuse will result in more children's being neglected by their parents and more adolescents'

---

1 James Q. Wilson, "Heroin," in *Thinking about Crime* (New York: Basic Books, 1975), p. 132.
2 Erich Goode, *Drugs in American Society*, 5th ed. (New York: McGraw-Hill, 1999), pp. 95, 333.
3 Ibid., pp. 333–4.

neglecting their education and other important developmental tasks.

Children need parents who are attentive and involved. If parents are oblivious to their children's needs, the effects on their children's future welfare, and indirectly on the rest of society, constitute significant harms. Adolescence, too, is a time when we learn important social and cognitive skills, habits, and forms of self-discipline that are crucial to our future ability to work, to succeed financially and professionally, to sustain important relationships, and to meet important family commitments, such as those to our children. If a person spends the adolescent years getting high on heroin instead of going to class, meeting the emotional challenges of growing up, and developing constructive relationships with adults in positions of authority, he or she is likely to be permanently hobbled.

Heroin may not necessarily have this negative effect on motivation. Drug researchers have observed that the effects of a drug vary with "set and setting": the social group in which the drug is used, their expectations and values, and the occasions on which the drug is used.[4] If, for example, alcohol is drunk in drams throughout the day as a refreshment for the purpose of giving workers a mental lift, it will predictably have a different psychological effect than if it is drunk after work in bars for the purpose of lowering one's inhibitions against making sexual advances or getting into fights. Within our society, however, heroin use is not part of any formal social setting, and its use is not regulated by conventional norms. Furthermore, it is widely understood to depress motivation and concern with conventionally defined success. So it is reasonable to expect that if heroin were now legalized, heroin use would continue to have this psychological effect, at least for the foreseeable future.

Since alcohol is currently legal, and this condition is not likely to change soon, it is necessary to defend the prohibition of any drug against the background of legalized alcohol. Observe, then,

---

4 See Norman Zinberg, *Drug, Set, and Setting: The Basis for Controlled Intoxicant Use* (New Haven, CT: Yale University Press, 1984).

that an increase in the use of some drug as a result of legalization might actually result in a net decrease in the independent harms of drug and alcohol abuse taken together. To understand why, suppose that people who are now deterred from abusing a drug by its relative scarcity and danger typically abuse alcohol instead. If so, then legalizing this drug might not result in a net increase in overall drug and alcohol abuse. It might only make drugs that are now illegal the "drug of choice" of those who now abuse alcohol. This is significant because alcohol abuse is arguably worse – the cause of more independent harms – than the abuse of any currently illegal drug. Heroin use, for example, does not cause liver cirrhosis or have the same apparent tendency to lead to violence. So if the legalization of heroin were to lead those who now abuse alcohol to abuse heroin instead, this might result in a net *reduction* of independent harms.

To be justified in supporting drug prohibition, while leaving current alcohol policy in place, we must therefore be justified in believing that the abuse of drugs that are now illegal would increase and that the number of independent harms overall would increase as a result. I think we are justified in believing this about heroin partly because of the uniquely intense form of pleasure it offers, which leads some of those who use it to "fall in love" with it in ways that they would never fall in love with alcohol or any other drug, and partly because habitual heroin use has a greater negative impact on motivation than habitual drinking typically does. For these reasons I believe that the independent harms of drug abuse would increase substantially if heroin were legalized.

To fill in this picture, imagine that anyone older than 18 or 21 may buy heroin from the local liquor store or the local pharmacy, in safe and inexpensive doses. Under these conditions we can safely predict that the amount of heroin use among the general population will rise, and that the amount of heroin abuse among parents and adolescents will rise proportionately. If heroin is legal, parents can buy and use it legally. Some of them will abuse it. Parental abuse of heroin will lead to the neglect of children, resulting in feelings of low self-esteem and a lack of direction. Parental drug use is also a model for child drug use. The greater availability of heroin will mean, too, greater availability to one's peers, and so more peer acceptance of heroin use, and so greater influence within peer groups to use it.[5] True, no one younger than 18 or 21 will be able to purchase heroin legally, but we can safely predict that this restriction will do no more to discourage underage heroin use than it does now to discourage underage drinking or smoking.[6] This is because, as is now the case with alcohol and cigarettes, some stores will not be particularly vigilant about to whom they sell their heroin, and many teenagers will be able to get heroin from older siblings or friends, or to steal it from their parents, or to have strangers buy it for them.

For these reasons, if heroin is legalized, some individuals will be at a *much higher* risk of heroin abuse than they otherwise would be: those whose parents and peers use it who would not otherwise use it, who have low self-esteem and a lack of direction as a result of parental neglect resulting from heroin abuse, who are struggling emotionally and academically, and who would therefore welcome this means of escape. To this we can add that adolescence is often a difficult period, as individuals struggle to form an independent identity and to accomplish important tasks amid an array of psychological distractions. For this reason, heroin will be tempting to adolescents in many different situations. Get high, and you can stop worrying about being unpopular, or unattractive, or bad at sports or worrying about your parents' finances or marital troubles. Given the relief from anxiety and worry that heroin temporarily provides, as well as the simple pleasure, the

---

5 See Denise B. Kandel, Ronald C. Kessler, and Rebecca Z. Margulies, "Antecedents of Adolescent Initiation into Stages of Drug Use: A Developmental Analysis," in Denise B. Kandel, ed., *Longitudinal Research on Drug Use: Empirical Findings and Methodological Issues* (Washington, DC: Hemisphere, 1978). For the relative influence of peers and parents in drug use, see Denise B. Kandel, "Adolescent Marijuana Use: Role of Parents and Peers," 181 *Science* 1067 (14 September, 1973).

6 See Substance Abuse and Mental Health Services Administration (SAMHSA), *Results from the 2002 National Survey on Drug Use and Health: National Findings* (Rockville, MD: Office of Applied Studies, 2003) (henceforth NSDUH 2002), figures 3.1 and 4.2, available online at www.samhsa.gov/oas/NHSDA/ 2k2NSDUH/Results/2k2results.htm, chap. 2, pp. 30, 36.

belief that *many* adolescents will be at a substantially higher risk of heroin abuse if it is legalized is thus reasonable. Perhaps most adolescents who abuse drugs have other problems beforehand, but legalization would only increase the likelihood that those with other problems would abuse drugs, thus exacerbating whatever other problems they already had.

Some defenders of drug legalization suggest that teen drug use is only increased by the "forbidden fruit" effect of prohibition. It is important to bear in mind, then, that although forbidden fruit may be sweeter to some, unforbidden fruit is still sweet, and people will therefore eat it if it is available. If merely forbidding something could motivate people to do it, parents and schools could improve their children's math scores by prohibiting them from doing their math homework.

In assessing the weight of the forbidden fruit conjecture, it is also important to bear in mind that few defenders of legalization maintain that sale to minors should be legalized, and if the sale to minors is prohibited, then the forbidden fruit effect remains, at least to some degree. Assuming, then, that this effect is real, legalization would surely result in an increase in drug use, since now it would be easier to get this fruit, which is allegedly so desirable because forbidden.

Should the sale of heroin to minors also be legalized, then, to reduce further the forbidden fruit effect of prohibition? Even if the sale to minors is legalized, this effect will presumably remain to some degree, since parents, schools, and the media will presumably continue to discourage heroin use. Should *all* authority figures remain neutral on teen heroin use, then, in order to reduce the forbidden fruit effect? The idea that this would *decrease* teenage heroin abuse seems as unrealistic as the belief that teenage pregnancy will decrease if parents, schools, and the media remain entirely neutral on the advisability of teenage sex. For one thing, heroin use, like sex, is a source of pleasure. For another, although it may be true that the "forbidden" status of heroin and sex enhances its appeal for some adolescents – those who are more rebellious or antiauthoritarian by temperament – surely it does at least as much to discourage others – those who seek their parents' and teachers' approval and accept their parents' and teachers' norms.

Students of drug abuse observe that many drug users "mature out" of a habit. This is presumably because, as one gets older, the pleasures of drug use no longer seem worth its costs. This judgment, however, must be due in large measure to the fact that drugs are illegal. Because heroin is illegal, it is relatively difficult, expensive, and unpleasant to acquire, and less safe to use. This "hassle factor" is one of the main reasons why people stop using heroin. Eliminate the hassle factor and people are much less likely to mature out of a habit.[7]

In any case the problem with drug abuse among young people is not primarily that this will inevitably result in habitual drug use for the rest of their life. It is that heavy drug use during this crucial stage of a person's development will close opportunities that will be difficult to reopen later on. If every child were rich or highly talented, the consequences of increased heroin abuse among adolescents might not be so bad. Teenage drug abuse might set some people back a bit, but, if they are rich, they will always have the opportunity to reapply themselves to their education, and if they are gifted, they will always have talents for which there is a high demand. Not every child is rich or gifted, however. Most of us need to work hard to master basic skills and habits during adolescence if we are to have a decent opportunity to succeed at the things we wish to do later on. Most of us need practice, and guidance, and an incentive to develop discipline, to master these basic skills. Secondary and college education cannot play this role in the life of students who are too busy getting high to attend class or do their homework. Heroin abuse during adolescence will thus have the practical effect of closing many valuable opportunities going forward that will take extraordinary effort or good fortune to reopen.

7 On the connection between the "hassle factor" and rates of use, see John Kaplan, *The Hardest Drug: Heroin and Public Policy* (Chicago: University of Chicago Press, 1983), p. 125; Erich Goode, *Between Politics and Reason: The Drug Legalization Debate* (New York: St. Martin's Press, 1997), p. 115; and Goode, *Drugs in American Society*, pp. 324, 354.

Some may think these concerns provide an argument only for drug education in primary and secondary school, but studies suggest that cognitive education about the effects of drugs does very little to reduce rates of drug use.[8] An alternative to prohibition is raising the price of heroin through taxation, which would certainly have an impact on teen drug use, all the more since most teenagers have less disposable income than adults do. But high taxation rates on alcohol and cigarettes are obviously compatible with substantial consumption by teenagers.[9] Furthermore, although alcohol is heavily taxed, alcohol consumption now is still well above Prohibition levels,[10] and that suggests that increasing price through taxation is not as effective in decreasing consumption as prohibition is. If we are serious, then, about protecting young people from the independent harms of drug abuse, we must be open to the possibility that prohibition is the best policy all things considered.

The Costs of Prohibition

The argument I have just sketched for heroin prohibition depends on a number of empirical assumptions that might be questioned. But even if they are sound, it does not directly follow that heroin prohibition is justifiable since this policy itself imposes substantial burdens. The most serious of these is the substantial risk of criminal liability that it imposes on those who are tempted to manufacture and sell heroin. If this risk of criminal liability is too great, then the benefits of reducing heroin abuse among parents and teenagers will not be great enough to justify prohibition. A defensible policy of prohibition therefore rests on the assumption that heroin abuse can be reduced substantially – enough to make

---

8 See Nancy Tobler, "Drug Prevention Programs Can Work: Research Findings," 11 *Journal of Addictive Diseases* 1 (1992); Richard R. Clayton, Anne M. Cattarello, and Bryan M. Johnstone, "The Effectiveness of Drug Abuse Resistance Education (Project DARE): 5-Year Follow-up Results," 25 *Preventive Medicine* 307 (1996); and Goode, *Drugs in American Society*, p. 366.

9 See NSDUH 2002, figures 3.1 and 4.2, pp. 30, 36.

10 Goode, *Drugs in American Society*, p. 186.

the policy worthwhile – even with a gradual and proportionate system of penalties that does not impose an unacceptably high risk of imprisonment on anyone.

What would such a system look like? First, the possession of small quantities of heroin would be a misdemeanor, not a felony. (Whether this amounts to *decriminalization* depends on whether legal penalties for misdemeanors and even less serious administrative violations are counted as "criminal" penalties.) Second, although the manufacture, sale, and possession of larger quantities would be a felony, the penalties would be gradual and proportionate. No one would be incarcerated for a first offense, unless he or she refused to meet the conditions of probation, such as counseling and community service, and penalties for second and third offenses would remain relatively light. Although it seems fair to confiscate supplies and other assets even for first offenses, long prison sentences for those involved in the drug trade are unjustifiable, even after the second or third conviction, because these sentences are themselves so destructive of a person's life prospects.

Some may now ask, Why should we go so soft on drug dealers? The big dealers are grown-ups who know what they are doing. Why should they not be subject to harsher penalties for selling drugs to kids? Why should they not be beheaded, as the former "drug czar" William Bennett reportedly once suggested?[11] The answer is that just as it is a choice to *sell* drugs, it is a choice to *use* them, and just as there are inner and outer pressures that might lead a person to *use* drugs against his or her own best interests, there are inner and outer pressures that might lead a person to *sell* them against his or her own best interests. So if the free choice to sell drugs seems to justify harsh penalties for doing so, the free choice to buy and use them seems immediately to undermine this justification. Some may wish to deny that heroin use is a choice because it is addictive, but, for reasons given in the next chapter, the addictive nature of drugs fails to support the judgment that it

---

11 Daniel Lazare, "The Drug War Is Killing Us," *The Village Voice*, 23 January 1990, p. 25.

is not an individual's choice to use them. The point, then, is that if the free choice to do something warrants society's letting the individual suffer the worst consequences of his or her actions, as the argument for harsh penalties suggests, then it seems society should likewise do nothing to prevent people from using heroin voluntarily, and so should not impose penalties on anyone for selling it to those who wish to do so.

Drug prohibition is justifiable only because we think that people, especially young people, do not always act in their own best interest and therefore need some protection from the worst possible consequences of their potentially imprudent decisions. Since this is equally true of many people who decide to deal drugs, especially young people, they likewise need protection in the form of a gradual and proportionate system of penalties. Some may contend here that heroin prohibition will be ineffective without a harsher system, but there is no compelling reason to believe that prohibition is made any more effective by harsh penalties than it would be by lighter penalties more reliably and consistently enforced.[12] In fact, the effectiveness of prohibition might be *increased* by lightening the penalties, since this might increase the chances of conviction for drug offenses by compassionate juries.

The risk of criminal liability is not the only significant burden imposed by a policy of drug prohibition. The drug trade is also violent because it is illegal, and so theft, breach of contract, unfair trade practices, and other disputes cannot be settled in court. Drug prohibition thus increases the risk of violence to those involved in the drug trade and to innocent bystanders. For this reason a policy of heroin prohibition will be fully justifiable only if the government is committed to reducing the neighborhood violence that the black market creates, where this will require, among other things, increased funding for neighborhood policing.

That the drug trade also produces huge profits for those willing to break the law has had grave political consequences in some countries, such as Colombia and Afghanistan, where drug lords

---

12 See James Q. Wilson and Richard J. Hernstein, *Crime and Human Nature* (New York: Simon & Schuster, 1985), p. 62.

wield tremendous political influence and inflict terrible violence on those who oppose them.[13] For this reason a policy of heroin prohibition will be fully justifiable only if the governments of the developed world are willing to offer financial incentives to less developed countries to grow other crops and to help them suppress money laundering activities. In some cases it may also be necessary for the governments of the developed world to use their military forces against drug lords, with the consent of local governments, in order to protect local government officials from intimidation and violence, and, in some places such as Afghanistan, actively to engage in a policy of "nation-building."

Another significant cost of drug prohibition is that its effective enforcement creates a risk of civil liberty violations by the police and others. If heroin prohibition is to be fully justifiable, drug enforcement agencies must therefore be trained to respect civil liberties scrupulously and institutional incentives must not be created for breaking the law in ways that violate the civil rights of innocent citizens.

Still another cost of drug prohibition is that it increases the risk of fatal overdose to those who now use drugs because illegal drugs are commonly sold in unpredictable and unregulated doses. To be fully justified in enforcing a policy of heroin prohibition, the government must therefore also be committed to reducing the risk of fatal overdose by effective public information activities. And, in order to reduce the risks of contracting hepatitis, HIV, and AIDS, the government should in any case make clean needles available to drug users who want them.

Another burden of heroin prohibition as it is currently enforced is that it prohibits the possession of heroin for the treatment of

13 For the negative effects of drug prohibition on other countries, see Jorge Chabat, "Mexico's War on Drugs: No Margin for Error," 582 *Annals of the American Academy of Political and Social Science* 134 (July 2002); Marlyn J. Jones, "Policy Paradox: Implications of U.S. Drug Control Policy for Jamaica," 582 *Annals of the American Academy of Political and Social Science* 117 (July 2002); and Fransico E. Thoumi, "Illegal Drugs in Colombia: From Illegal Economic Boom to Social Crisis," 582 *Annals of the American Academy of Political and Social Science* 102 (July 2002).

pain. Heroin is thought by some to be more effective than other drugs in treating chronic pain caused by diseases such as cancer because it relieves a person's misery while allowing her to maintain relatively clear conscious contact with the world. If so, then a defensible policy of heroin prohibition must also allow the prescription of heroin for use in hospitals and hospices.

In sum, heroin prohibition as it is now enforced imposes many burdens. Some of these, such as overly harsh penalties, are unjustifiable, but these unjustifiable burdens are not *necessarily* imposed by a policy of heroin prohibition. What I maintain, then, is that if the unnecessary burdens of heroin prohibition are eliminated, and the necessary burdens are therefore lightened as much as possible, the benefits of reducing heroin abuse among parents and young people can justify a policy of heroin prohibition. Of course prohibition also deprives some people of a safe and easy supply of heroin for the purpose of responsible recreational use, but for reasons that I give in the next chapter I believe this burden can also be justified.

The Individualistic Structure of the Argument

My argument for heroin prohibition can now be summed up as follows:

1. Heroin prohibition reduces heroin use compared to what it would be if heroin were legal, because legalized heroin would be easier, safer, and more pleasant to acquire, and less expensive and safer to use.
2. Heroin prohibition, because it reduces use, also reduces abuse.
3. If heroin were legalized, its abuse would therefore increase not only among mature adults who could buy it legally, but also among teenagers and young adults.
4a. Since heroin abuse among parents will damage the future prospects of their children, by reducing parental motivation to care for their children properly, an increase in heroin abuse among parents will increase the risk to their children of significant losses.
4b. Since heroin abuse among adolescents will damage the future prospects of some by reducing their motivation to accomplish

crucial developmental tasks, an increase in heroin abuse among them will increase their risk of significant losses.

5. Heroin prohibition would substantially reduce heroin abuse among parents and adolescents, even if it were enforced by a gradual and proportionate system of penalties with a scrupulous respect for civil liberties.

6. On these assumptions, the reasons for some young people to want to be protected from an environment in which heroin is legal outweigh the reasons of others to want to be in an environment where heroin is legal (provided that the external costs of violence and intimidation that arise from the drug trade can be defrayed by more funding and other changes in policy).

7. This suffices to justify heroin prohibition from the moral point of view.

Assumptions (1) to (5) are empirical assumptions. I have offered some reasons to accept them, and I will offer more reasons in Chapter 9. My primary aim, though, is not to defend these empirical assumptions. It is to argue that if (1) to (5) are true, then (6) is true, and if (6) is true, then (7) is true. That is, I want to defend (6), given these empirical assumptions, and then argue that the truth of (6) is sufficient to establish (7).

Given the degree to which my argument for heroin prohibition depends upon empirical facts, some may think that it is a utilitarian argument. Utilitarianism, which directs the government to adopt policies that will maximize happiness over time, is commonly criticized on two grounds. First, it is said, happiness is not the only thing that individuals have good reason to want from their government; among other things, they also have good reason to want the government to ensure that they have a fair share of resources and opportunities (even if having less than a fair share would not decrease their happiness). Second, even if happiness were the only thing that individuals have good reason to want from government policies, happiness might be *maximized* in the aggregate by policies that violate individuals' moral rights. Happiness might be maximized in the aggregate by a system of slavery that enslaves only a small minority, for example. If my argument for heroin prohibition were utilitarian in nature, it might therefore be open to these two objections.

Regardless, however, of the merit of these two objections to utilitarianism, my argument for heroin prohibition is not utilitarian in this sense. It does not assert or assume that heroin prohibition will maximize happiness in the aggregate. It asserts instead that, given certain empirical assumptions and the satisfaction of other conditions, the risk of lost opportunities that some individuals would bear as the result of heroin legalization justifies the risks of criminal liability and other burdens that heroin prohibition imposes on other individuals. The legalization of heroin would create a social environment – call it the *legalization environment* – in which some children would be at a substantially higher risk of irresponsible heroin abuse by their parents and in which some adolescents would be at a substantially higher risk of self-destructive heroin abuse. There are good reasons for these individuals to want to avoid these risks, and so to want not to find themselves in this environment. Any good reason for a person to prefer her situation under some government policy is, in my view, a reason of *some* weight for the government to adopt this policy, and if there is a personal reason of this kind in favor of a government policy, then, in my view, this policy is morally justifiable unless there is a good personal reason against this policy – a good reason for someone to prefer his situation without this policy – that has at least as much moral weight. Given, then, that there are good reasons for some people to prefer their situations in a prohibition environment, heroin prohibition is morally justifiable if these reasons have greater weight than anyone's reasons to prefer his or her situation in a legalization environment. Of course there *are* good reasons for people to prefer their situation in a legalization environment, since heroin laws create risks and other burdens, particularly the risk of criminal liability. If, however, the risks created by a prohibition environment can be contained in the ways I sketched in the previous section, then I believe that the reasons that some individuals have to prefer their situation in a prohibition environment outweigh the reasons anyone has to prefer his or her situation in a legalization environment.

This is not a utilitarian argument that claims that happiness will be maximized in the aggregate by heroin prohibition. It is an individualistic argument that claims that the worst risk to some individual under heroin legalization is worse than the worst risk to some individual under prohibition, provided that the penalty structure is gradual and proportionate. There is no talk here of maximizing happiness in the aggregate. Indeed, if we assume that happiness consists in either pleasure or desire satisfaction, as utilitarians have historically maintained, heroin prohibition might well fail to maximize happiness and yet still be justified by the individualistic argument I have just sketched.

Some may think that an individualistic defense of heroin prohibition, which is based on a comparison of individuals' risks and not on a comparison of aggregated harms, is doomed from the outset, because a policy of drug prohibition imposes a risk of imprisonment on people, and imprisonment at an early stage of one's life is worse for one's life prospects than heroin abuse is. If prison is worse than heroin abuse, then the strongest reasons for a person to prefer his situation in a legalization environment seem to have greater weight than the strongest reasons anyone has to prefer her situation in a prohibition environment, in which case the individualistic argument for prohibition fails.

The weight, however, of a person's reasons to prefer his situation under a policy of prohibition or legalization depends on the degree of risk that the relevant policy imposes on him ex ante – at the moment he is born, say – and not on how bad the worst *possible* outcome is for him under this policy. After all, dying of a heroin overdose that one would not have suffered had heroin been illegal is worse than going to prison, but from this it does not directly follow that heroin prohibition is justified, because the risk to anyone of a fatal overdose that is created by a policy of legalization might still be too small to justify the corresponding risk to anyone of criminal penalties. Likewise, although being imprisoned as a young person may be more destructive of one's life prospects than abusing heroin typically is, that a person's reasons to prefer a legalization environment have greater weight than anyone's reasons to prefer a prohibition environment does not directly follow. This is because, given a gradual and proportionate system of penalties, the *risk* of imprisonment that the prohibition environment creates is not so high, and, given the various opportunities that such a system would create to avoid the worst outcome of imprisonment, this system would give individuals adequate control over this outcome.

The general point I am making here is familiar from other kinds of risk comparison. By driving to a restaurant to meet friends on a Saturday night we increase our risk of dying in a car crash, and dying in a car crash is worse than dining at home alone. It does not follow, though, that our reasons not to drive to the restaurant outweigh our reasons to do so. Since the risk of dying is not so high ex ante, or before we start to drive, and it can be managed at least to some degree by how we choose to drive, our reasons to want to drive to the restaurant outweigh our reasons to stay home.

Observe, too, that similar judgments about comparative risk must be made in order to justify laws that we all endorse within any individualistic, nonaggregative moral framework. Consider, for example, the argument for laws against theft that our reasons to want our property to be made more secure by laws against theft outweigh other people's reasons to want to be free to take from us whatever they want when they want it. In general, being imprisoned is worse than being stolen from, but it does not follow that laws against theft cannot be justified. This is because a person's reasons to want to live in an environment where there is a lower risk of theft may have greater weight than anyone's reasons to want to live in an environment in which he or she can take things from others without their permission without incurring any risk of imprisonment.

An important objection to drug laws is that their enforcement has resulted in the imprisonment of a large number of young black males in poor inner-city neighborhoods. This objection is typically made against cocaine prohibition, and particularly against laws that prohibit dealing crack, since most young black male drug offenders are in prison on cocaine charges. But the kind of policy of heroin prohibition that I am defending here might also be thought unfair because it would place a higher risk of imprisonment on black kids in the inner cities than it would on white kids in the suburbs. Disadvantaged youth have an especially strong incentive to sell drugs in order to improve their material conditions because their material conditions are relatively poor. The risk of criminal liability imposed by prohibition on disadvantaged youth is therefore especially high. Furthermore, the ability to make money by dealing drugs may lead some young people to drop out of school, and that creates reasons to oppose prohibition that are related to some of the very same concerns that I have offered to justify it. Ironically, it is an implication of these objections that prohibition also benefits poor youth by providing them with the opportunity to make substantial amounts of money from an illegal enterprise. Given the choice between flipping burgers legally for minimum wage and making $50 an hour selling illegal drugs, many of us would opt for the latter. The objective value, however, of this entrepreneurial opportunity does not seem great enough to justify the corresponding risk of criminal liability and educational truancy. This is partly because the money this opportunity provides rarely constitutes a lasting benefit for the drug dealer, and partly because imprisonment, especially at a relatively early stage in one's life, is so destructive of one's life prospects. For these reasons, it is certainly reasonable to wonder how the burdens of drug control policy on inner-city youth can be morally justified.

Part of the answer is that a substantial rise in inner-city heroin abuse would be particularly bad for inner city youth.[14] Not only are the educational opportunities of disadvantaged children worse in general because their schools are worse. They are also worse because their surrounding culture does less to encourage them to do well in school. We have all heard about how academic achievement is discouraged by peer groups in inner-city schools. Imagine how much more discouraged from educational performance students would be in a culture of heroin abuse. Imagine too how much less likely middle-class voters would be to

14 Goode, *Drugs in American Society*, pp. 115–16.

fund improvements in inner-city education over the long run if inner-city kids were to be perceived as a bunch of heroin addicts. One anecdote from Ronald Reagan in the 1980s about a "welfare queen" seems to have forced even Democrats to pledge "to end welfare as we know it." How much more damage would the widespread perception of heroin addiction among inner-city youth do to undermine a national commitment to equality of educational opportunity over time?

Some readers will surely feel uneasy about any attempt to justify the burdens of drug control policy on poor inner-city youth by its benefits to *them*. So it is important to understand that my claim here is not that a person who wishes to make money by selling drugs is herself benefited by a higher risk of criminal liability. It is that some kids – those who will be at a much higher risk of significant losses within a legalization environment – are sufficiently benefited by drug control to justify the risks that a prohibition environment imposes on *other kids* who are tempted to deal drugs. We need not justify criminal laws, whether drug laws or laws against theft, by their benefits to those who will be tempted to do what these laws prohibit; these laws can be fully justified instead by their benefits to *others*, whom they function to protect in some way.

The judgments I have just made about the relative weight of various benefits and burdens may of course be questioned. My primary goal in what follows is not to defend these judgments, but to argue that if they are sound, then drug prohibition can be justified as compatible with the fundamental principles of contemporary liberalism. Some may think that drug prohibition is wrong because it is moralistic, or because it is paternalistic, or because it violates individuals' moral rights to liberty. What I hope to show is that heroin prohibition can be defended against these objections *if my assumptions are correct*. What I hope to show, in other words, is that the *only* serious moral question in evaluating drug prohibition is whether the kind of judgments I have made about the relative weight of the relevant benefits and burdens are sound. If they are, then heroin prohibition is morally justifiable. If they are not, then it is not.

Douglas Husak contends in Part I that the criminalization of drug use can be justified only if a person who uses drugs deserves to be punished, and he seems to criticize my defense of drug prohibition on the ground that it fails to show how the individual user deserves punishment.[15] To this one might respond that a person *legally* deserves to be punished provided he or she has broken a valid law, one that has been enacted and enforced through the proper political and legal procedures. If a policy of drug criminalization is properly adopted and properly enforced, those convicted of drug use or possession therefore deserve to be punished in this sense. But what Husak means, I think, is that criminal punishment is justified only when a person *morally* deserves to be punished, and, although he does not make this explicit, I suspect he believes that a person morally deserves to be punished only if he or she has actually *wronged* someone in some way. His objection, then, to the criminalization of drug use is that no one wrongs anyone simply by using a drug and therefore no one morally deserves to be punished for doing so.

The first point to make in response is that I am not here defending the criminalization of heroin *use*, but only the criminalization of the *manufacture and sale* of heroin, and for the possession of quantities above a certain size, a gram, say. I agree with Husak that no one wrongs anyone simply by using heroin, and therefore that no one morally deserves to be punished for doing so, and I also agree that the use and possession of small quantities of heroin should not be treated as felonies, though for different reasons. The position that I am defending here is therefore not open to the objection that it advocates punishment simply for using drugs, which no one morally deserves.

This clarification, however, does not completely dispose of the objection, since someone might maintain as well that no one morally deserves to be punished simply for making drugs or selling them to a willing buyer, and so hold that criminal penalties for the manufacture and sale of heroin are also morally unjustifiable. The second point to make, then, is that there is no compelling

15 Husak, this volume, Part I, Chapter 2.

reason to accept this principle of justified punishment or to agree that the government may impose criminal penalties only for actions for which a person morally deserves to be punished. Sometimes the government is justified in imposing criminal penalties for conduct that does not directly wrong or harm anyone because this policy is nonetheless necessary to protect people effectively from harm. This seems true, for example, of criminal penalties for the private possession of high-powered military weapons. A private weapons collector does not *wrong* anyone simply by *possessing* such weapons, provided she or he is careful that they do not fall into the wrong hands. But criminal penalties for possessing such weapons may nonetheless be justified by the goal of ensuring that these weapons do not fall into the wrong hands, provided that these penalties are fair and proportionate.

"Punishment," Husak admonishes, "is the worst thing that our state can do to us," and so there must be "compelling reasons" for the state to punish us.[16] If, however, we identify "punishment" with the imposition of *any* criminal penalty, then it is misleading to say that *punishment* is the worst thing our state can do to us. This is because although *some* criminal penalties are certainly terrible – death, life imprisonment, and even a short term in any maximum-security facility – other criminal penalties, such as probation and mandatory counseling and community service, are not so bad. This is not to deny that that the government must have "compelling reasons" to impose any criminal penalty on us, but, in my view, there *is* compelling reason for drug prohibition provided that my claims about the relevant benefits and burdens are correct. Hence there may be compelling reason for the government to impose criminal penalties for dealing drugs even if no one *morally deserves* to be punished for doing so because no one *wrongs* anyone in doing so.

The third point to make in response to Husak's apparent objection to my argument for drug prohibition is that he himself seems to reject the general principle that the government is justified in imposing criminal penalties only on those who morally deserve

16 Ibid.

to be punished. This is because in his concluding chapter on drug legalization he allows that criminal penalties for violating laws regulating the manufacture and sale of drugs might be justified as reducing overall harm,[17] and because, as he himself argues in Chapter 2,[18] it does not follow from the fact that a law can be justified as reducing overall harm that any one *morally deserves* to be punished for violating this law. This is not to charge Husak with any inconsistency. His view, as I understand it, is that the freedom to use drugs is highly valuable, and that limiting this liberty therefore imposes a substantial burden that requires a strong justification, and that no reason that does not involve the claim that people are wronged by the exercise of this freedom will in fact be strong enough. The freedoms to manufacture and sell drugs, on the other hand, are not so valuable, and so these liberties may be limited for weaker reasons. On this last point, at least, we seem to agree.

17 Ibid., Chapter 5.
18 Ibid., Chapter 2.

7   Drug Prohibition and Liberalism

Is Prohibition Objectionably Moralistic?

A common objection to drug prohibition is that it is "moralistic." This is to say that drug prohibition imposes a moral belief that some hold on others who do not hold it, and the content of this belief is that drug use is morally wrong even if it does not put anyone at serious risk of personal injury. Some may believe that drug use is morally wrong in this way because it involves the mistreatment of one's mind – as nonprocreative sex might be thought to involve the mistreatment of one's sexual organs – and they may support drug laws for this reason. If this were the only reason for drug prohibition, I think this policy would be completely unjustifiable.

The argument that I have just offered for heroin prohibition is not moralistic in this sense. It does not assume that drug use is wrong or bad per se. It assumes that using drugs is the wrong thing for *some* people to do because *their* drug use is irresponsible or imprudent, and that their drug use is irresponsible or imprudent *because it has bad consequences* and not because it is *intrinsically* wrong. Nor does my argument assume that drug use is irresponsible or imprudent for *everyone*. I believe to the contrary that, in most instances, drug use is a perfectly defensible form of enjoyment, and nothing I have said so far should be taken to be inconsistent with this belief. My argument here is not that drug use is wrong or bad *in itself*, but that *sometimes* drug *abuse* leads to *harm* that is *serious enough* to be the legitimate object of government concern, and the prevention of which may therefore justify drug prohibition on certain empirical assumptions and conditions.

Related to the charge that drug laws are moralistic is the thought, more common among academic philosophers, that they are "perfectionist." These laws might be thought to be perfectionist because their basic aim might seem to be to discourage people from engaging in an activity that is degrading to them in impeding the full development and exercise of their higher human capacities: the capacities for theoretical and practical reasoning, aesthetic discrimination and enjoyment, spiritual insight and growth, love and friendship, and so on. The best life for humans, one might think, is one in which we fully develop and exercise these capacities in our activities. Drug use, or at least heavy drug use, impedes the full development and exercise of these capacities and so, the thought goes, should be discouraged for this reason.

Personally I agree that the best life for us is one that develops and exercises our higher human capacities fully. This, however, is not the argument for heroin prohibition that I have just sketched. My argument is that the legalization of heroin would substantially increase the risk to some individuals of losing important opportunities, the loss of which would significantly dim their life prospects. This argument presupposes that heroin abuse is degrading in one sense: that it interferes with the full development and exercise of a person's capacity for practical reasoning, either by weakening one's ability to make sound judgments about the best thing for one to do or by weakening one's motivation to act in accordance with these judgments. But it is not the degradingness of heavy heroin abuse in this sense that *alone* justifies prohibition; prohibition is justified instead as preventing the loss of important opportunities that *results* from this kind of degradation.

James Q. Wilson, a leading defender of drug prohibition, has defended his opposition to drug legalization by the following claims: that heavy drug use is "destructive of human personality,"[1] that it "destroy[s] the user's essential humanity"

1 James Q. Wilson, "Heroin," *Thinking about Crime* (New York: Basic Books, 1975), p. 156.

and "alters the soul,"[2] that it results in the "degradation of human personality,"[3] and that it is "destructive of human character."[4] I believe these claims are best understood to mean that heavy drug use thwarts the development and exercise of the human capacity for practical reason in the ways I have just identified. This is because Wilson uses the terms *human personality, humanity, soul,* and *character* to refer to "those natural sentiments of sympathy and duty that constitute our human nature and make possible our social life,"[5] and this is simply the naturalistic or Humean way of referring to our capacity for practical reasoning. For this reason I think Husak is wrong to suggest in Part I that Wilson's reasons for drug prohibition are "religious."[6] I also think that Erich Goode is wrong to characterize Wilson's defense of drug prohibition as purely moralistic on the grounds that it is nonconsequentialist.[7] This is because the "destruction of character" that Wilson refers to is in fact an empirical consequence of drug abuse. Is there is any disagreement, then, between Wilson and me on the proper justification of drug prohibition? Perhaps we differ on whether degradation in this sense can *alone* justify drug prohibition. I suspect, however, that Wilson would agree with me that it is not *merely* the degradation of heavy drug use that justifies prohibition, but the degradation *together with* the bad consequences of this degradation. Thus in the same essay in which he charges that drug abuse results in the "degradation of human personality," he also observes that those who are so degraded "regularly victimize their children by neglect, their spouses by improvidence, their employers by lethargy, and their coworkers by carelessness."[8]

---

2 Wilson, "Against the Legalization of Drugs," 89 *Commentary* 26 (February 1990).

3 Ibid., p. 28.

4 Wilson, "Drugs and Crime," in Michael Tonry and James Q. Wilson, eds., *Drugs and Crime* (Chicago: University of Chicago Press, 1990), p. 523.

5 Wilson, "Against the Legalization of Drugs," p. 26. See, too, Wilson, "Drugs and Crime," p. 523, for related thoughts.

6 Husak, this volume, Part I, Chapter 3, Drugs and Immorality.

7 Erich Goode, "Thinking about the Drug Policy Debate," in James A. Inciardi, ed., *The Drug Legalization Debate*, 2d ed. (Thousand Oaks, CA: Sage, 1999), p. 115.

8 Wilson, "Against the Legalization of Drugs," p. 24.

In denying that my defense of heroin prohibition is objectionably *moralistic* or *perfectionist*, I do not deny that it is *paternalistic*. It is paternalistic in the sense that it justifies limiting the liberty of young people to buy heroin by the benefits of this policy to them. In the next section I will defend the moral permissibility of this kind of paternalism. The claim here is simply that, although paternalistic in this sense, my argument is not objectionably moralistic or perfectionist.

Some may doubt that it is possible to state a paternalistic argument that is not fundamentally perfectionist. To understand why, suppose that motorcyclists should be required to wear a helmet because with a helmet they are less likely to die or suffer permanent brain damage in a motorcycle accident. We care about permanent brain damage because without a functioning brain, a person is unable to enjoy life, to be educated, to find satisfying work, to foster a loving family, and to develop in other areas such as sports or the arts. This paternalistic argument for motorcycle helmet laws may therefore seem perfectionist because it assumes that certain activities and capacities have value, both in themselves and for what they make possible, and that any life that lacks these activities and capacities is therefore impoverished in important ways.

If, however, this kind of paternalism were genuinely perfectionist, then many *nonpaternalistic* policies that we support would likewise be perfectionist. Consider, for example, a policy of wealth redistribution that is justified as promoting equality of educational opportunity. Equality of educational opportunity, as I understand it, is achieved when each person has the education she needs to compete on fair terms for certain goods, such as wealth, desirable occupational positions, further education, and other socially valued achievements. Understood in this way, equality of educational opportunity is a morally compelling ideal only if the goods to which it promotes fair access are of genuine value. In advocating equality of educational opportunity as a morally important goal, we must therefore assume that a life without these goods is in some ways poorer or worse for the person whose life it is. So if the paternalistic argument for motorcycle helmet laws is perfectionist, then so, it seems, is the nonpaternalistic equality-of-educational-opportunity argument for redistributive taxation.

Neither the paternalistic argument for motorcycle helmet laws nor the nonpaternalistic egalitarian argument for redistributive taxation is genuinely perfectionist, in my view, because neither presupposes the validity of any *specific* conception of the best kind of life for humans. These arguments do not presuppose that the best life for us is a life of theoretical reasoning and contemplation, as Aristotle thought; or of inner tranquility, as Epictetus thought; or of Christian piety, as Saint Paul thought. These arguments do not even presuppose that we should strive to develop and exercise our higher human capacities as fully as possible. To the contrary, these arguments are fully compatible with a wide range of beliefs about what is most worthy of pursuit: a life of theoretical inquiry, inner tranquility, Christian piety, the pursuit of money or power, sensual pleasures, and so on. Since the same can be said of my argument for heroin prohibition, this argument is also not genuinely perfectionist, in my view.

Some may characterize perfectionism more broadly than I do, and, on some possible characterization, heroin prohibition may be a perfectionist policy even if it is adopted on the grounds I have given. But if heroin prohibition is perfectionist on some interpretation, we must still ask, What, if anything, makes perfectionism on this interpretation *objectionable*? Perfectionist justifications for coercive government policies seem objectionable, I think, largely because they presuppose that some things are good for people who do not want them or who do not think they are valuable or important. The argument for equality of educational opportunity seems unobjectionable, then, even if it is in some sense perfectionist, because most people do want, or at least will want when they are older, certain opportunities that a decent education makes possible. But if this is right, then the paternalistic arguments for motorcycle helmet laws and heroin prohibition are likewise unobjectionable. This is because most people will also want a functioning brain and the emotional and educational development necessary to achieve important goals in adulthood. To the extent, then, that persons are at a greater risk of losing these goods where it is legal to ride without a helmet or to buy heroin, there are reasons, identified by their own current or future preferences, to want the relevant paternalistic restrictions.

Another reason to think that perfectionist policies are objectionable is that they violate the liberal principle of government neutrality, that the government should remain as neutral as possible toward different conceptions of a good life.[9] In a pluralistic society such as ours, the thought goes, individuals endorse different ideals of the best life a person could lead. A modern democratic government should therefore remain neutral on which ideal is sound and so should enforce only those policies that are, in some sense, neutral toward these different conceptions of how it is best to live.

Some may believe that drug prohibition is objectionably perfectionist because it violates this principle of neutrality, but I believe to the contrary that it does not. One might think that a government policy is objectionably nonneutral whenever it provides unequal benefits to two different persons as a consequence of the fact that they hold different conceptions of the good. If so, then drug prohibition would violate the principle of neutrality because it burdens those whose conceptions of the good place value on getting high on drugs in a way that it does not burden others. This, however, cannot be the correct interpretation of neutrality, since many perfectly neutral policies also provide greater benefits to some as a consequence of the fact that individuals hold different conceptions of a good life. Murder laws, for example, burden serial killers in a way that they do not burden the rest of us. To have a coherent and feasible ideal of neutrality, we must therefore say that a policy violates the principle of neutrality only when it is adopted *for nonneutral reasons*. Since murder laws are adopted for the neutral reasons of safety and security, this policy is therefore neutral in the relevant sense even if it has unequal benefits for individuals holding different conceptions of the good life.

---

9 For the classic statement, see Ronald Dworkin, "Liberalism," in *A Matter of Principle* (Cambridge, MA: Harvard University Press, 1986).

If this is the correct understanding of the principle of neutrality, we may say that a government policy is neutral in the relevant sense if it is adopted for and can be fully justified by neutral reasons alone. Which reasons are these? A fully satisfactory general account is difficult to provide, but as a rough approximation one can say that a reason for the government to endorse a policy is neutral if (a) it is provided by or it is equivalent to some genuine interest that individuals have in the government's endorsing this policy, by which I mean that it is provided by or is equivalent to some good reason for individuals to prefer their *own* situation when the government adopts this policy; (b) this interest is important; and (c) this interest is itself a part of, or is grounded in some other interest that is a part of, the best secular justification for policies that liberals and progressives widely endorse, such as equality of educational opportunity. The reason for murder laws that they reduce the risk of unwanted death is neutral, then, because it is identified by our interest in not being unwillingly killed; this interest is important; and it is part of the best secular justification for murder laws, which liberals and progressives all endorse.

I believe that the reasons I have given for heroin prohibition are also neutral in this sense. First, they are identified by the interests that children and adolescents have in not being in an environment in which heroin is easily available. Second, these interests are important, given the impact that heroin abuse by their parents or by them at this crucial stage of their development will have on their future prospects. Third, these interests are grounded in the interests that we have in developing certain habits and mastering certain skills as adolescents and young adults that are part of the best secular explanation of why we care about equality of educational opportunity, which is a fundamental commitment of liberalism and progressivism. A policy of heroin prohibition justified in the way I have proposed is therefore neutral in the morally relevant sense, and objection to this policy as moralistic or perfectionist on the ground that it violates the liberal principle of neutrality is an error.

Is Prohibition Objectionably Paternalistic?

I have just explained why I do not think that my argument for heroin prohibition is objectionably moralistic or perfectionist, and why I think a policy justified in this way would satisfy the liberal principle of neutrality. Here I will add that this policy, as I have defended it, is also not "conservative" or "authoritarian" or "puritanical." The justification for heroin prohibition, in my view, is provided by the liberal goal of ensuring that each individual has adequate opportunities upon entering adulthood to achieve the good things in life, broadly conceived. Its purpose is not to enforce a social hierarchy, or to encourage commitment to traditional religious views or ways of life, or to encourage moral purity or asceticism. Nor is its purpose to enforce law and order or compliance with policy directives from above. To the contrary, I believe the rationale for heroin prohibition that I have offered is thoroughly progressive in spirit.

My defense of heroin prohibition is paternalistic, however, and some may think that it is morally objectionable on this ground. So I should now explain why I do not think this kind of paternalism is morally objectionable.

To say that a coercive policy is paternalistic is to say that it limits the liberty of individuals for their own good. What does it mean, though, for the government to limit a person's liberty "for her own good"? It might mean that government officials are actually motivated by concern for the welfare of those whose liberty the policy limits. Or it might mean that the only sound justification for this policy is that it advances the welfare of those whose liberty it limits. Unfortunately, neither interpretation provides a fully satisfactory account of the distinction between paternalistic and nonpaternalistic policies.

To see why, suppose that what makes a policy paternalistic is that government officials are actually motivated to adopt this policy for paternalistic reasons. It follows from this analysis that a policy might be paternalistic even if there is sufficient nonpaternalistic reason for it. Suppose, for example, that government officials are motivated to adopt highway speed limits for the paternalistic reason that each driver will be safer if he or she is required to drive more slowly. Then speed limits are paternalistic, according to this analysis, even if a convincing nonpaternalistic case can be made: that each driver will be safer if *other drivers* are required to drive more slowly. This is odd. Why should the *policy* be paternalistic, as opposed to the aims of some legislators in supporting it, if there is sufficient nonpaternalistic reason for it?

If, on the other hand, we suppose that a policy is paternalistic if and only if the only sound justification for it is paternalistic, then it follows that every genuinely paternalistic policy is justifiable. This is because, if the only sound justification for a policy is paternalistic, then there *is* a sound justification for it, and the policy is therefore justifiable. This leaves no room for the thought that paternalistic policies are morally objectionable precisely *because* they are unjustifiable. One might suggest in response that a policy is paternalistic if and only if the *best*, or most persuasive, justification for it is paternalistic. But this leaves no room for the thought that paternalistic policies are wrong because paternalistic reasons are *especially* bad reasons, because, say, they are illegitimate. This is because, from this point of view, the best or most persuasive justification will *never* be a paternalistic one, and so, on this analysis, no policies will actually *be* paternalistic.

In light of these difficulties, it seems we should understand the notion of a paternalistic policy in another way. I will say that a policy is genuinely paternalistic if and only if two conditions are satisfied: (a) There is insufficient nonpaternalistic reason for it, and (b) the government has this policy only because someone in the relevant political process – legislative, judicial, executive – counts some paternalistic reason in its favor. According to this definition, no policy for which there is sufficient nonpaternalistic reason is therefore genuinely paternalistic, no matter how government officials are motivated, and paternalistic policies might be justifiable or not, depending on whether paternalistic reasons are ever morally sufficient to justify the government in limiting a person's liberty.

An important consequence of this analysis for drug policy is that heroin prohibition might not be a paternalistic policy even if the paternalistic argument I have given is the strongest one and this policy is adopted for this reason. This is because some nonpaternalistic reason in its favor might also be sufficient to justify it. To illustrate, suppose, as I also believe, that heroin legalization would result in a substantial increase in the number of parents who use heroin habitually, and so in a substantial increase in children who are neglected as a result. Suppose that protecting children from this kind of neglect suffices to justify this policy. Heroin prohibition would then not be paternalistic, as I have just characterized paternalism, because the limitation of parental freedom that it imposes could be fully justified, not by reference to the *parents'* welfare, but by reference to the welfare of their children.

I will now set this possibility aside and assume, for the sake of argument, that if heroin prohibition is justifiable, it is only on the paternalistic grounds that I have offered – because none of the nonpaternalistic arguments in its favor suffice – and that this policy is therefore genuinely paternalistic, in my sense, because it is supported by government officials on the basis of this paternalistic argument. I make this assumption in order to consider whether being paternalistic in this way would constitute a decisive objection to this policy, and so to explain why I do not think it would.

Paternalistic curtailment of a person's liberty is morally justifiable, in my view, if the good reasons there are for this person to prefer her situation when her liberty is limited in this way outweigh the good reasons there are for her to prefer her situation when her liberty is not limited in this way. I think this is true of heroin prohibition. That is, I think the reasons for some young people to prefer their situations when heroin is illegal outweigh the strongest reasons for them to want it to be legal, and I think this is true even if these young people disagree and so would actually prefer their situations if heroin were legal. This is because, in my opinion, the objective reasons there are for a person to prefer her situation when she is less likely to abuse heroin in ways that will seriously damage her life prospects objectively outweigh the objective reasons there are for her to want this form of recreation to be more easily available to her during this period of her life.

(In speaking of "objective" reasons here and of their "objective" weight, I mean to imply that something might be good or bad for a person even if she does not believe that it is, and even if she would not believe this upon informed reflection, and that how good or bad something is for a person is likewise independent of her beliefs.)

Many arguments have been made against government paternalism over the years: that it is not the government's business to protect people against themselves; that no one could rationally consent to give the government this kind of political authority; that a person cannot wrong himself by his own voluntary actions: that government officials are never epistemically justified in believing that a person is better off when his liberty is limited against his will; that paternalism stunts human individuality and so human development; that paternalistic interference is inherently insulting or demeaning, to name just a few. I find none of these arguments persuasive, but this is not the place to explain why. Instead I will consider what I take to be the *strongest* reason to think that paternalistic interference is generally unjustifiable, in order to explain why I do not think this reason provides a decisive objection to the kind of paternalistic policy of heroin prohibition that I am defending here.

Government paternalism is harder to justify in general than nonpaternalistic coercive government policies because it is generally within a person's control whether or not to do things that risk her own future well-being, whereas it is not generally within a person's control whether or not *other people* do things that risk her own future well-being. To illustrate, consider the relative weight of the reasons that Jones has to want her own freedom to drive fast to be curtailed and the reasons that Jones has to want Smith's freedom to drive fast to be curtailed. Since it is within Jones's own control how fast she drives, whereas it is not within Jones's control how fast Smith drives, Jones's reasons to want the government to prohibit Smith from driving fast have greater weight than her reasons to want the government to prohibit her from driving fast. This illustrates the way in which, given paternalistic and nonpaternalistic reasons of similar content or reasons that are related to the same goods or goals, the nonpaternalistic reasons have greater weight, because of the difference in control over the actions that pose the relevant risks. As a consequence of this difference in weight, paternalistic interference is more difficult to justify in general than nonpaternalistic interference is.

Few of us, however, would agree that the fact that an activity is within a person's control entails that her reasons to want the freedom to engage in this activity outweigh the reasons for her to want to be prohibited from doing so. So consider the New York statute limiting bakers' hours that was struck down in the notorious *Lochner* decision.[10] Although it was in the control of bakers not to work more than 60 hours a week – since they could have quit or refused to work longer hours and accepted the consequences – many of us think their combined reasons of health and job security to want their own hours to be limited by law outweighed their reasons to want to be free to work longer hours. Many of the bakers presumably thought so, too. This shows that the mere fact that it is within one's control not to do an act that will impose a risk of harm on oneself does not entail that one's reasons to want to be prohibited from doing this act are too weak to justify the government in limiting one's liberty in this way.

There is an important difference, though, between *wanted* paternalism, which limits a person's liberty in a way that he wants because he sees this policy as being to his advantage, and *unwanted* paternalism, which limits a person's liberty in a way he does not want because he does not see this policy as being to his advantage. The New York law limiting bakers' hours was justifiable, some may think, only because it was wanted. Unwanted paternalism, in contrast, is always wrong, they may believe, precisely because it limits a person's liberty for his own good "against his will," as Mill put it.[11]

What would justify such a distinction between wanted and unwanted paternalism? Given the great value that some place on

---

10 *Lochner v. New York* 198 U.S. 45 (1905).
11 J. S. Mill, *On Liberty*, ed. Elizabeth Rapaport (Indianapolis: Hackett, 1978), p. 9.

personal autonomy, they may think that the fact that a person believes that it is in her best interest to do something is always a morally weighty reason for this person to object to any policy that prohibits her from doing it. Call this a *reason of self-direction* against government interference with her freedom of action. Given the relative weakness of the reasons for anyone to want the government to limit her liberty to do something, a weakness due to the fact that it is within her control not to do it, advocates of personal autonomy may believe that reasons of self-direction against government interference always decisively outweigh the paternalistic reasons in its favor, and that unwanted paternalism is therefore never justifiable. Wanted paternalism, in contrast, is sometimes justifiable because there are no reasons of self-direction against the limitation of liberty that it involves, and so none to outweigh the relatively weak paternalistic reasons in its favor.

Although considerations of this kind may succeed in showing that unwanted paternalistic interference with the liberty of fully mature adults is generally unjustifiable, I do not think they succeed in showing that the paternalistic argument I have given here for heroin prohibition fails. This is because both the weight of the reasons of self-direction against government interference *and* the degree to which the factor of control weakens a person's reasons to want the government to limit her liberty vary significantly with a person's ability to reason about what is best for her to do. If this were not the case, it would make no sense to allow, as virtually every antipaternalist does, unwanted paternalistic interference with the freedom of children to do things that are harmful to them.

What makes paternalistic interference with the liberty of children seem justifiable is that children do not have a clear understanding of the consequences of their actions for their future well-being; they do not understand the shape of a normal human life, the wants and needs that one will have as one gets older, and the way imprudent actions now can permanently put one at a disadvantage in achieving goals one is likely to have later. Since this is also true of many adolescents, though to a lesser degree, paternalistic interference with their liberty is also easier to justify.

Because adolescents are generally less skilled than mature adults at weighing the negative consequences of their actions, the fact that an adolescent believes it to be in his best interest to do something generally has less weight as a reason of self-direction against government interference with his freedom to do it. Moreover, under these conditions, the fact that an adolescent can control whether or not to engage in some activity does less to weaken the reasons there are for him to prefer his own situation when he is prohibited from engaging in an activity that is potentially harmful to him. Consequently, although unwanted paternalistic interference with the liberty of adults whose mental capacities are fully mature may be generally unjustifiable for the reasons I have just given, it does not follow that the paternalistic policy of heroin prohibition that I have proposed is likewise unjustifiable, since its intended beneficiaries are teenagers and young adults.[12]

For this reason, too, I believe my defense of heroin prohibition is compatible with the principle of antipaternalism that Mill defends in *On Liberty*. This is because immediately after first stating this principle, Mill goes on to qualify its application by making clear that "it is meant to apply only to human beings in the maturity of their faculties."[13] Mill is not specific about when, in his view, human beings achieve this important state, but it is certainly arguable that most of us do not in fact achieve the maturity of our faculties, in the sense relevant to the evaluation of paternalism, until well into our twenties, if then. For certain legal purposes, such as marriage, driving, voting, and drinking, the

---

12 Since individuals are at the highest risk for drug abuse in their late teens and early twenties, this group is also the most important target of drug control from a purely quantitative point of view. See Kevin Chen and Denise B. Kandel, "The Natural History of Drug Use from Adolescence to the Mid-Thirties in a General Population Sample," 85 *American Journal of Public Health* 41 (January 1995); and Substance Abuse and Mental Health Services Administration (SAMHSA), *Results from the 2002 National Survey on Drug Use and Health: National Findings* (Rockville, MD: Office of Applied Studies, 2003) (henceforth NSDUH 2002), figure 2.3, available online at www.samhsa.gov/oas/NHSDA/2k2NSDUH/Results/2k2results.htm, chap. 2, p. 22.

13 Mill, *On Liberty*, p. 9.

law may set the age of adulthood at 14, 16, 18, or 21. It does not follow, though, that all, or even most, individuals actually reach the relevant maturity of their capacity for practical reasoning at those ages. So if we interpret the relevant idea of maturity as involving a full understanding of the shape of a normal life, one's likely future needs and wants, and the consequences of one's actions in adolescence for one's ability to satisfy these needs and wants later on in life, then the policy I am proposing is consistent with Mill's principle of antipaternalism. Of course Mill may have meant something different by "the maturity of the faculties." Since, however, this is what real maturity of the faculties consists in, it is the maturity that is actually relevant to moral assessment of the permissibility of paternalism.

Kant, another great liberal, maintained that "paternal government" is fundamentally illegitimate.[14] What he meant, though, by "paternal government" is a government that undertakes a comprehensive direction of the lives of its subjects in order to maximize their happiness, according to the government's own conception of what their happiness consists in. By adopting a paternalistic policy of heroin prohibition, the government does not undertake anything so comprehensive or intrusive as "paternal government" in this sense. For one thing, the purpose of this policy, as I have described it, is not, strictly speaking, to promote anyone's *happiness*, but to protect certain important *opportunities*. For another thing, the aim of this policy is not to regulate a person's life in accordance with any general conception of happiness that the government adopts and wishes to impose; rather it is simply to discourage a certain activity that may have lasting bad consequences for a person's well-being as he himself might understand it later in life. Finally, this policy is fully compatible with the essentials of a democratic constitution: freedom of speech, freedom of religion, freedom of association, political liberty, freedom of movement, and freedom to own personal property. Since

14 See Immanuel Kant, "On the Proverb: That May Be True in Theory, but Is of No Practical Use," in Ted Humphrey, trans., *Perpetual Peace and Other Essays* (Indianapolis: Hackett, 1983), p. 73.

the recognition and protection of these liberties prevent paternal government in Kant's sense, any form of paternalism, for instance, heroin prohibition, that is compatible with the recognition and protection of these important liberties is therefore compatible with Kant's view that paternal government is fundamentally illegitimate.

The Relevance of Addiction

I have just explained why I believe that a policy of heroin prohibition can be justified as benefiting young people whose liberty it limits, and why this position is compatible with liberalism, as historically understood. But I have left open whether paternalistic interference with the liberty of older persons can be justified. It might be thought that it can be because heroin is addictive. The reason to oppose paternalism, some may think, is that it conflicts with or undermines our autonomy. Since, the thought continues, heroin addiction also undermines our autonomy, paternalistic interference with heroin use by mature adults is therefore justifiable.

I have so far said nothing about the addictiveness of heroin because it does not play a central role in my argument for prohibition. Far more relevant in my view is the negative impact that habitual heroin use will have on the cognitive, emotional, and social development of young people. But the addictiveness of heroin seems relevant to assessing the paternalistic argument for heroin prohibition since it seems to bear on both the strength of reasons of self-direction to oppose restriction and the relevance of control as a factor in weakening a person's reasons to favor restriction. So in this section I want to consider the extent to which the addictiveness of heroin bolsters the paternalistic case for prohibition.

When it is said that a drug, such as heroin or cocaine, is addictive, at least seven different things are commonly meant. One (1) is that this drug is *physically* addictive. When the amount of the drug in one's body decreases, one experiences unpleasant withdrawal symptoms, such as chills, fever, diarrhea, nausea, vomiting, and bodily aches and pains. In this sense, alcohol is addictive because its heavy use is sometimes followed by delirium tremens. Cocaine, by contrast, is not addictive in this sense.

Another thing (2) that is meant by saying that a drug is addictive is that it is a "strong positive reinforcer": that because the use of the drug is very pleasurable, normal human beings are motivated to use the drug again and again, if they have the opportunity, and even, in some cases, to overcome significant obstacles to do so. Another way to characterize this second sense of *addictiveness* is to say that that the experience of using the drug gives rise to what T. M. Scanlon calls a "desire in the directed-attention sense."[15] Having experienced the pleasure of drug use, one's mind continues to focus on this pleasure as a reason to use this drug again and to take this reason to be a good one (even if "in a cool hour" one also judges that it is not). In this sense, cocaine is highly addictive, and many other things are too, although to a lesser extent. Chocolate, for example, is addictive in this sense, since the memory of the pleasure of eating a piece leads many of us to want to eat another one.

Another thing (3) that is meant by saying that a drug is addictive is that those in the habit of using this drug experience some form of psychological distress when they stop using it, particularly the mental state of *craving*. In this sense nicotine is addictive, since a smoker will crave a cigarette after some time has elapsed since his last one and feel unsettled and dissatisfied without one.

Still another thing (4) that is meant by saying that a drug is addictive is that people commonly develop a psychological dependency on it because of the feelings of well-being it creates or the relief from stress, anxiety, or negative feelings about oneself that it provides. In this sense, exercise can also be addictive, since those who get emotional relief from exercise commonly devote much of their free time to it for this reason.

Another thing (5) that may be meant by saying that a drug is addictive is that those who develop a psychological dependency

15 T. M. Scanlon, *What We Owe to Each Other* (Cambridge, MA: Harvard University Press, 1998), p. 39.

on it, because of the feelings of well-being it creates or the relief from stress it provides, tend to feel ashamed of themselves for depending on it or for giving in to the temptation to use it for these reasons. In this sense, pornography may be addictive for some people.

Another thing (6) that is meant by saying that a drug is addictive is that because of the pleasure and psychological relief that it provides people have difficulty controlling its use: They use more than they had intended to use, or they use the drug even though they had genuinely intended not to. An important factor here is the phenomenon of "weakness of the will": Even though a person sincerely believes on due reflection that he should not do something, and this belief remains stable upon further reflection, the contrary intention to do this thing nonetheless continues to form in his mind and to motivate him to act. There are different ways in which this phenomenon might be understood. We might understand it as a situation in which a person's rational judgment is "overpowered" by some more primitive emotional or appetitive mammalian motivational system. Or we might understand it as a situation in which a person has inconsistent beliefs – that there is sufficient reason to do something and also that there is sufficient reason not to do it – and, whatever the underlying cause, the first belief leads this person to form the effective intention to do this thing, even though he continues to affirm the second belief upon reflection. However we understand it, this phenomenon is familiar enough and identifies an important way in which drug use is difficult to control. In this sense activities other than drug use, for example, gambling, are also addictive.

Finally, what we may mean when we say that a drug is addictive is (7) that because of the pleasure and psychological relief it provides, people will choose to use this drug even when this use results in the loss of other things of greater value for them, and that its use is therefore "irrational" in this substantive sense. We can say that one thing has greater value for a person than another when having it contributes more to her life's going well (for her) over all. If someone chooses to use a drug because of the pleasure or psychological relief this provides even when this results in her sacrificing things that have greater value – job, family, friendships, health, savings, and self-respect – then its use is "irrational" in the substantive sense intended here, and this is another way in which this drug may be addictive. Other activities such as sex and gambling can also be addictive in this way.

When we identify a drug such as heroin as addictive and intend this description to distinguish its use from other activities, we may mean to claim that it is addictive in *all seven ways*. So it is worth pointing out that many other activities are addictive in at least one of them, and some are addictive in all. Indeed, the concept of addiction does not mark a sharp distinction between heroin and alcohol, since alcohol is also addictive for some people in all seven ways, although perhaps not to the same degree.

Although many activities are addictive in one or more of these ways, however, and some are addictive to some degree in all of them, not all seven aspects of addiction are equally relevant to the justification of legal paternalism. The mere fact that an activity, for instance, eating chocolate, is pleasurable, for example, and so leads people to want to do it again does not in itself strengthen the paternalistic case for its prohibition. Nor does the fact that an activity such as exercise is a central activity in a person's life for the feelings of well-being it creates. The fact that ceasing an activity will result in physical withdrawal symptoms or that it will produce the state of craving may provide reasons of minimal weight for prohibiting it, as may be true of the fact that a person feels ashamed of indulging his appetite for this activity. But these reasons seem far too weak to justify anything as burdensome as legal coercion. So none of these ways of being addictive seems highly relevant to the justification of paternalistic interference.

If an activity is difficult to control, however, this characteristic does seem to strengthen the case for paternalistic interference. Paternalistic interference is more difficult to justify in general, I have said, because normally it is within a person's control not to do what will harm her. If an activity is addictive in the sixth sense, then a person will find it difficult to control it through the exercise of her own considered judgment, and her reasons for wanting the government to interfere with her freedom to engage in it will therefore have greater weight. Furthermore, if it is difficult for a person to control through her own considered judgment whether or not to engage in an activity, then her reasons of self-direction to want the government not to interfere with her freedom to engage in it have less weight. In fact, under these circumstances the value of self-direction may actually be *promoted* by government interference. Hence when an activity is addictive in the sixth sense, the value of self-direction may seem to warrant government interference rather than providing a decisive objection against it.

Still, the fact that it is difficult for a person to control whether or not she will engage in an activity does not alone seem to provide a sufficiently weighty reason for the government to prohibit her from doing it, because the activity may not be very harmful. Imagine someone who finds himself compulsively checking the price of his stock on the Internet every few minutes when he is alone in his office even though he has no plans to sell. The mere fact that it is difficult for this person to control his curiosity about the current value of his stock provides a reason of very little weight for government interference, because checking stock prices on the Internet, even compulsively, is not very harmful.

Paternalistic interference with a person's heroin use is justifiable only when its use is likely to *harm* her. Furthermore, it is justifiable only when the probable costs to her of using heroin decisively outweigh the probable benefits to her of using it. For this reason, I think that paternalistic interference with a person's heroin use is justifiable only when that use is addictive in the seventh sense. Given the fact that a person's heroin use is substantively irrational in this way, the fact that it is difficult to control further strengthens her reasons for wanting the government to protect her against herself, and so is relevant to the paternalistic case for restriction. The difficulty of control *alone*, however, is insufficient to justify this policy.

If a person is more likely to use heroin if it is legalized, and her use of heroin will be addictive in the sixth *and* seventh ways, then I think this is a good reason for her to want the government to adopt a policy of prohibition. The question is whether this reason suffices to justify a policy of paternalistic interference with the freedom of mature adults to use heroin, given the burdens this policy will impose on them and others. There are really two distinct questions here. First, is the fact that a mature adult will be more likely to use heroin if it is legalized and that heroin will be addictive for her in the sixth and seventh ways if she uses it, a sufficient reason *for her* to prefer her situation when the government restricts her freedom to acquire heroin, given the burdens this places on *her*? Second, is this fact sufficient to justify the burdens on *others* that a policy of prohibition will impose?

I believe the answer to the first question is yes. If a mature adult is more likely to use heroin if it is legal, and her use of heroin will be difficult for her to control and substantively irrational, then, assuming that the independent harms that will result are substantial, I believe that this is sufficient reason for her to prefer her situation when heroin is prohibited, and so harder for her to get, assuming that the penalties for possession of small quantities are light. If so, it is not surprising that so many addicts oppose legalization.[16] A policy of prohibition will be effective, however, only if selling heroin is also prohibited, and this policy will be effective only if the penalties for the sale of heroin are substantial. The answer to the second question depends, then, upon whether the paternalistic reasons for the government to adopt a policy of prohibition in order to protect mature adults from the independent harms of heroin abuse have enough weight to justify the burdens this policy will impose on others who will be tempted to sell heroin when it is illegal.

I do not think they do. The greater ability of mature adults to understand the consequences of their actions and to make sound judgments about what is best for them on the basis of their empirical and deliberative experience means that they have a weaker claim to governmental protection against the negative consequences of their own voluntary actions. Furthermore, as a person grows older, his unwise choices are more and more expressive of his own settled character and less and less a consequence of

16 Wilson, "Heroin," p. 135.

immaturity. I do not believe that these differences in deliberative capacity and expressive significance are great enough to justify a sharp distinction between paternalistic regulations aimed at benefiting teenagers and those aimed at benefiting young adults. But I do think they are great enough to justify a distinction between paternalistic regulations that are aimed at benefiting young adults and those that are aimed at protecting those who have reached the full maturity of their faculties, assuming their mental capacities to be normal.

Bear in mind here that the paternalistic case I have made for heroin prohibition is based on a delicate balance of the interests of young people in being protected from self-destructive heroin use and the interests of others in being protected from criminal liability and other burdens. Because this balance is delicate, the relevant differences between young adults and fully mature adults are great enough, in my opinion, to make a policy of prohibition unjustifiable by its benefits to fully mature adults even though it is justifiable by its benefits to young people.

Some may believe to the contrary that heroin prohibition is justified by its benefits to mature adults because once a person uses heroin, whatever his age, he is "hooked," because he cannot stop using it without agony, and because habitual heroin use turns a person into a zombie with no capacity for genuine self-direction. This picture, however, has little basis in reality. For one thing, although heroin is certainly addictive in the seven ways described, a large proportion of those who use the drug do not develop a self-destructive habit.[17] For another thing, those who develop a habit may nonetheless stop without great suffering. (The discomfort involved in kicking a habit is commonly likened to having the flu for a few days.) Finally, although habitual heroin use can be bad for a person in depressing his motivation, it does not turn a

17 See Lee N. Robins, "Drug Use by U.S. Army in Vietnam: A Follow-up on Their Return Home," 99 *American Journal of Epidemiology* 235 (1974); Norman E. Zinberg, "Nonaddictive Opiate Use," in Robert L. DuPont et al., eds., *Handbook on Drug Abuse* (Rockville, MD: National Institute on Drug Abuse, 1979); Erich Goode, *Drugs in American Society*, 5th ed. (New York: McGraw-Hill, 1999), pp. 324–6; and NSDUH 2002, p. 57.

person into a zombie whose capacities for rational self-direction are no longer functioning at all.

Except when one is the victim of direct external compulsion, a person's actions are voluntary in the sense that they are governed by his intentions, which in turn are generally governed by his judgments about what it is best for him to do. It is an error based on science fiction to think that heroin addiction turns a person into a zombie who is completely unable to guide his actions by his own deliberative judgment. Heroin use may be *difficult* for some people to control in the ways described, but this does not mean that it is entirely *outside* their control. This is because a person always has the mental capacity to *decide* to stop using heroin or to form the intention to do so. Because heroin is addictive in the sixth sense, this intention may not be entirely effective. Thus although one may genuinely intend at 9:00 A.M. not to use heroin that day, one may nonetheless decide at 4:00 P.M. to use it because the idea of getting high suddenly seems so appealing. But a person also has the mental capacity to decide to do what she needs to do in order to succeed in acting in accordance with her original intention – to form the intention to get whatever help she needs to stay clean that day, for example. Forming and acting on these intentions to seek help will be more difficult without the right kinds of social support, and this is good reason for the government to support treatment programs to help those who want to do so to stay clean. But I do not believe that the difficulty for some mature adults of quitting heroin without the right kind of support provides a sufficient reason for the government to impose criminal penalties on others for selling it to them.

As I have already mentioned, the burden of criminal liability is not the only burden relevant to assessing heroin prohibition. Among the other burdens I have mentioned is that prohibition makes heroin use less safe, because when heroin is illegal it is not sold in standard dosages, and so overdosing on it unintentionally is easier. The fact that heroin is addictive in the sixth and seventh senses makes this burden even heavier because it makes people more likely to buy heroin from dealers they do not know and so more likely to buy heroin of uncertain purity and strength, which is less safe to use. If the addictiveness of heroin strengthens the paternalistic case for prohibition, it therefore also strengthens the case for legalization.

Some may think that the addictiveness of heroin warrants legalization on this ground alone, but I do not agree. The risk of fatal overdose is not created solely by prohibition. This risk is *inherent* in heroin use because the amount of heroin that will kill a person is not so much greater than the amount it takes to get high.[18] Those seeking to get high by using increasingly large doses of heroin will therefore generally run *some* risk of fatal overdose, even if it is a small one. This means that the increase in the use of heroin that would result from legalization would also increase the risk of fatal overdose for some people: those who will use it if and only if it is legal. And *this* risk will be *increased* for some people by the addictiveness of heroin. Furthermore, the ready availability of heroin would also increase the risk of death to people who are depressed by providing an appealing means of suicide. Of course, if a person is better off dead, this is no reason for him to prefer his situation when heroin is harder for him to obtain. But some suicidal people are better off staying alive, and there is therefore good reason for them to prefer their situations when fewer appealing means of suicide are available. For these reasons, the health risks that legalization would increase seem to me to offset the health risks that prohibition creates.

Does Prohibition Violate the Rights of the Responsible Recreational User?

Heroin prohibition is justified, in my view, by its benefits to young people. This is because, according to me, the reasons for some young people to prefer their situations in a prohibition environment in which they will be at a lower risk of self-destructive heroin abuse and in which their parents will be less likely to abuse heroin irresponsibly outweigh the reasons of others to prefer their situations in a legalization environment, in which they

18 Goode, *Drugs in American Society*, p. 327.

will be at a lower risk of criminal liability if they choose to sell it, assuming that the system of penalties is gradual and proportionate and other conditions are met. A policy of prohibition, however, not only burdens those who would manufacture and sell heroin, but also burdens those who would enjoy using heroin and who would use it prudently and responsibly, by making heroin less available, more expensive, and less safe to use.

Not all heroin users are addicts (in the sixth and seventh senses). In fact, it is arguable that a majority of heroin users now use heroin responsibly as a way to relax and enjoy, even though its use is illegal. According to the Substance Abuse and Mental Health Services Administration (SAMHSA), 53 percent of those who used heroin in the past year could be classified as having a dependence on heroin or as having abused it.[19] However, this study applies the criteria for substance dependence and abuse specified in the *Diagnostic and Statistical Manual of Mental Disorders* (*DSM-IV*), and these criteria allow that a person may be "dependent" on heroin without having any significant personal problems or causing any significant harm to others.[20] It is thus unclear from the SAMHSA report what percentage of heroin users are actually *abusing* this drug. Furthermore, although this report concludes that 166,000 Americans used heroin in the month before the survey, the Office of National Drug Control Policy (ONDCP) concludes from this same report that twice that number (404,000) used heroin in the year prior to the survey, and that well over 20 times that number of Americans older than age 12 (3.7 million) have used heroin at least once in their life.[21] Taken together these observations suggest that only a minority of heroin users actually abuse it.[22]

19 NSDUH 2002, p. 57.
20 *Diagnostic and Statistical Manual of Mental Disorders*, 4th ed. (Washington, DC: American Psychiatric Association, 1994), pp. 181–3.
21 See here the "Drug Facts" section on heroin on the Office of National Drug Control Policy (ONDCP) Web site (2004), available online at www.whitehousedrugpolicy.gov/drugfact/heroin/index.html, p. 1.
22 Goode, *Drugs in American Society*, pp. 315, 324–6, claims that the vast majority are occasional users.

This is significant because recreational heroin use provides relaxation and enjoyment, which are good things. We all want relief from the frustrations and anxieties of our daily life. Heroin can free us temporarily from these negative feelings; it can, temporarily, put us in a better mood and therefore has value as a means of controlling our moods. In making heroin difficult to acquire, more expensive, and less safe, heroin prohibition therefore imposes a burden on those who would otherwise benefit from using it recreationally. Furthermore, if heroin is legalized, it is likely that only a minority of those who would not have used it under prohibition will now abuse it in a way that has lasting bad consequences for them or others. A policy of heroin prohibition thus arguably sacrifices the liberty of the many for the benefit of the few, and some may believe that for this reason this policy violates our moral rights.

The idea that we have moral rights comes to life historically against the background of certain kinds of domination and oppression, such as absolute monarchy and slavery. There are moral limits, we think, to what the government may do to us in advancing the interests of a family dynasty or of a ruling class. These moral limits we call *rights*. More recently the idea that we have rights has gained significance against the background of utilitarianism, according to which the government should act so as to maximize happiness. Some policies, such as throwing the Christians to the lions for the entertainment of the Roman masses, might maximize happiness in the aggregate by sacrificing the individual. To explain what is wrong with such policies we say they would violate individuals' moral rights.

The thought that we have rights that might be violated by policies that maximize utility in the aggregate rests fundamentally, I believe, on a form of reasoning that I call *individualism*. Individualism requires that we evaluate the moral justifiability of government policies, or of the general moral rules or principles that properly regulate government conduct, by making one-to-one comparisons of the benefits and burdens that these policies, or rules or principles, would provide to or impose on individuals. Individualism thus forbids us to evaluate policies, or rules or principles, solely by considering their net aggregated benefit, or their net benefit summed over individuals, and permits us to endorse a policy or principle only if its benefit to some individual is great enough to offset the worst burden its adoption or observance imposes on someone. This explains, for example, why it would be wrong for the government to establish and maintain a system of slavery, even if this system would maximize individual welfare in the aggregate. Since this system would impose a burden on the individual slave that is substantially greater than any benefit someone would gain from this policy, individualism prohibits the government from adopting this policy.

Individualism is an essential component of the most influential contemporary theories of political rights. It is essential to John Rawls's view, for instance, that the government should observe principles that would be chosen by rational individuals in "an original position of equality" behind "a veil of ignorance."[23] This is because, not knowing "behind the veil" what specific situation she is in within her society, each individual will reject any principle that places a substantial burden on someone unless someone would bear a burden that is at least as great when this principle is not observed. Individualism is also essential, I think, to Ronald Dworkin's view that the government must treat all persons with equal concern and respect.[24] This is because the government will treat a person with equal concern and respect in adopting a policy that burdens her only if someone would be burdened at least as heavily by the absence of this policy. Individualism is also essential to Scanlon's view that the government should observe principles of conduct that no one could reasonably reject as the basis of informed, unforced agreement.[25] This is because a person can reasonably reject a principle of government conduct that benefits someone if and only if the government's observance of this principle places a burden of some sort on her that is worse

23 John Rawls, *A Theory of Justice* (Cambridge, MA: Harvard University Press, 1971), pp. 11–12.
24 Ronald Dworkin, *Taking Rights Seriously* (Cambridge, MA: Harvard University Press, 1978), pp. 272–3.
25 Scanlon, *What We Owe to Each Other*, p. 4.

than the worst burden someone would bear if the government were not to observe this principle.

The particular form of individualism that I adopt as the basis for evaluating whether a coercive government policy violates our rights to liberty is given by a principle I call the *burdens principle*. According to this principle, the government violates a person's moral rights in adopting a policy that limits her liberty if and only if in adopting this policy the government imposes a burden on her that is substantially worse than the worst burden anyone would bear in the absence of this policy. To say that a policy imposes a burden on someone is simply to say that there is sufficient reason for her to prefer her situation when the government does not adopt this policy. To say that a person bears a burden in the absence of this policy is simply to say that there is sufficient reason for her to prefer her situation when the government does adopt this policy. The burden imposed by a policy is substantially worse, then, than the worst burden anyone would bear in its absence if the reasons for one person to prefer her situation without this policy have substantially greater weight than the strongest reasons anyone has to prefer her situation with this policy in place.

The burdens principle represents an individualistic, non-aggregative approach to evaluating whether government policies violate our rights to liberty. It does not, however, prohibit the government from limiting the liberty of the many for the benefit of the few. This is because the reasons that the few have to want the government to limit the liberty of the many may have greater weight than the reasons the many have to want their liberty not to be limited. Consider, for example, the reasons for 19th-century African Americans to prefer their situation when slavery was constitutionally prohibited. This policy limited the liberty of the white majority to own black slaves, but it was nonetheless justifiable in line with the burdens principle, since the reasons for African Americans to want their enslavement to be constitutionally prohibited had vastly greater weight than the reasons anyone had to want the legal opportunity to own them.

Applying the burdens principle now to the policy of heroin prohibition, suppose that the reasons for someone to prefer her situation when heroin is illegal are at least as weighty as the strongest reasons anyone has to want heroin to be legal. Suppose, that is, that the reasons for someone to prefer her situation in a prohibition environment are at least as weighty as the strongest reasons anyone has to prefer her situation in a legalization environment. Then, according to the burdens principle, heroin prohibition does not violate anyone's moral rights, even if it limits the liberty of the many for the benefit of the few.

Some may protest here that there is an obvious difference between prohibiting slavery and prohibiting heroin, namely, that slavery violates individuals' moral rights whereas manufacturing and selling heroin do not. If, however, the burdens principle is the correct theory of our rights to liberty, as I believe it is, then legally enforced slave codes violate individuals' moral rights precisely by virtue of the fact that they impose a burden on someone in legally limiting his or her liberty that is substantially worse than the worst burden anyone would bear in the absence of this policy. If, then, this is *not* true of heroin prohibition, this policy does *not* violate anyone's moral rights.

A natural objection to the burdens principle is that it makes heroin prohibition too easy to defend. This is because it follows from this principle that if no one's reasons to want heroin to be legal have *substantially greater weight* than the weightiest reasons for anyone to want it to be prohibited, then the policy does not violate anyone's rights. Some may wish to hold instead that a coercive policy violates a person's rights if the reasons she has to want her liberty not to be limited have *slightly more weight* than the reasons anyone has to want her liberty to be limited. Or they may hold that a coercive policy violates a person's rights if the reasons she has to want her liberty not to be limited are *at least as weighty* as the reasons anyone has to want her liberty to be limited, provided, at least, that she is in the majority. I resist either of these alternatives because I think the government does something as seriously wrong as violating a person's moral rights only when its reasons for limiting her liberty are *decisively* outweighed by this person's reasons to want her liberty not to be limited, as the burdens principle requires.

It is not necessary, though, to rest my case for heroin prohibition on the validity of the burdens principle, which may seem arbitrarily biased toward the permissibility of various coercive government policies. It is possible to defend heroin prohibition instead by arguing that it satisfies a less permissive principle, which I will call the *individualistic principle of sufficient reason*. According to this principle, there is morally sufficient reason for a government policy that limits a person's liberty if the reasons for someone to want the government to limit a liberty in some way have greater moral weight than anyone's reasons to want the government not to limit this liberty in this way. If there is sufficient reason for a policy as judged by this principle, then, in my view, it violates no one's rights. The argument for this is simple. A policy violates a person's moral rights only if the government would wrong her in adopting this policy. The government wrongs a person in adopting a policy only if her reasons to want the government not to adopt this policy have greater moral weight than anyone's reasons to want the government to adopt it. So if the reasons a person has to prefer her situation when the government adopts a policy have greater moral weight than anyone's reasons to prefer her situation without this policy, then this policy wrongs no one and so violates no one's moral rights.

What I claim in favor of heroin prohibition is that the reasons of at least one person to prefer her situation in a prohibition environment outweigh everyone else's reasons to prefer his or her situation in a legalization environment, assuming that the penalties are gradual and proportionate and other relevant conditions are met. If so, then the policy does not violate the individualistic principle of sufficient reason and so, in my view, violates no one's moral rights.

The objection raised at the beginning of this section is that a policy of heroin prohibition violates the rights of those who would enjoy heroin and who would use it prudently and responsibly by making it more difficult for them to acquire safe and inexpensive heroin. I do not deny that this is a burden. The question is whether this burden is too heavy to be justified. I do not think it is. Pleasure, relaxation, and release from anxiety are certainly good things. An effective means of controlling one's mood and lifting one's spirits is also good. Heroin, however, although it is a source of a particularly intense form of pleasure, is not the only source of pleasure and relaxation available to us. Nor is it the only means of controlling our moods and lifting our spirits. There are also reading, art, music, exercise, and companionship, not to mention alcohol, food, sex, gambling, and prescription drugs. Heroin prohibition thus leaves many other sources of pleasure and means of psychological relief and mood control legally available to us. Furthermore, the policy of prohibition that I am defending here would treat the possession of small quantities of heroin as a misdemeanor and not as a felony. One reason for this is that although there is good reason to believe that the prohibition of the manufacture and sale of drugs functions to depress drug use substantially, there is also good reason to suspect that the criminalization of use does not have this beneficial effect.[26] So the benefits of criminalization are arguably too small to justify the burdens of criminal liability and the financial costs of enforcement. But another reason not to criminalize heroin use is that its use does have genuine psychological benefits, and some people may feel they need to use it in order to enjoy life or to cope with its difficulties. Heroin prohibition does not make heroin completely unavailable; it simply makes it harder to acquire and less safe to use. Since, then, a policy of prohibition would not completely remove the opportunity to use heroin, and it does not require a person who wishes to use it to risk imprisonment by doing so, I believe the benefits of protecting young people from irresponsible and self-destructive use can justify the burden of heroin prohibition on the responsible recreational user.

Another burden of heroin prohibition that is often mentioned by advocates of legalization is that enforcing it costs a lot of money. The costs of prohibition would be reduced if the government were to legalize some drugs, such as marijuana; and if it were to cease to

---

26 See Robert J. MacCoun and Peter Reuter, *Drug War Heresies: Learning from Other Vices, Times, and Places* (Cambridge: Cambridge University Press, 2002), pp. 72–100.

prosecute possession as a felony; and if it were to shorten prison terms for dealing drugs. But the cost of any effective drug policy would remain high. For one thing, effective enforcement with lighter penalties will require more frequent arrests and successful prosecutions. For another, if drug prohibition is to be fully defensible, more money must be spent to reduce the violence in poor neighborhoods that results from the drug trade and to combat the negative effects of drug prohibition on the government and civic life of foreign countries.

The expense of drug prohibition is another way in which this policy burdens the many for the benefit of the few, but I find this argument for legalization even less compelling than the objection that it unfairly burdens the prudent and responsible recreational user. If the funding of drug prohibition were to decrease anyone's quality of life substantially, then this policy would arguably violate the burdens principle on this ground. Under any equitable system of taxation, however, the cost of drug control will be distributed to all taxpayers, and those required to contribute the most will also be the ones whose quality of life will be least affected by the added burden of doing so. For this reason I believe the financial costs of drug control are morally justifiable within the individualistic moral framework that I endorse here.

In this section I have denied that someone's moral rights are violated whenever the government burdens the many for the benefit of the few, but I am not claiming that the numbers do not matter to the evaluation of government policies. If the greatest burden that heroin prohibition places on someone is at least as great as the greatest benefit that it gives to someone, and more individuals bear the greatest burden than receive the greatest benefit, then I think this policy is unjustifiable, and unjustifiable because it burdens more people than it benefits. My argument for heroin prohibition thus depends on the assumption that the greatest benefit to someone of prohibition is *significantly greater* than the greatest burden that prohibition imposes on anyone, or that the strongest reasons for someone to prefer her situation in a prohibition environment are *significantly weightier* than the strongest reasons for anyone to prefer his situation in a legalization environment (when the penalties are gradual and proportionate and other conditions are met). This assumption may certainly be challenged, but I have tried to explain here and in the final section of the previous chapter why I think it is true.

Drawing the Line

One of the main arguments I have given for heroin prohibition is admittedly paternalistic, and a common objection to paternalism is that drawing a principled distinction between those forms of (unwanted) paternalism that are justifiable and those that are not is not possible. This objection is commonly made by asking the rhetorical question "But where do you draw the line?" The implication is that since there is no principled basis for making a distinction between justifiable and unjustifiable forms of (unwanted) paternalism, one cannot coherently believe that one form is justifiable without thinking they all are. So if one thinks that any form of unwanted paternalism is justifiable, one is committed in principle to the legitimacy of Kant's "paternal government."

This objection, however, relies on the erroneous assumption that it is more difficult to draw a morally defensible distinction between justifiable and unjustifiable paternalistic policies than it is to draw a morally defensible distinction between justifiable and unjustifiable *nonpaternalistic* policies. Consider, to illustrate, the distinction between a *nonpaternalistic* law prohibiting offensive political speech, which most civil libertarians would oppose, and a *nonpaternalistic* law against the defamation of private citizens, which many civil libertarians would support. A distinction between these two kinds of regulation of speech is neither arbitrary nor incoherent because there are important differences between them. For one thing, the reasons individuals have to want the freedom to express their political views in an offensive manner have greater moral weight than the reasons individuals have to want the freedom to defame private individuals. For another thing, the reasons of private individuals to want to be protected from defamation have greater moral weight than the reasons of individuals to want to be protected from hearing political speech that angers or offends them. But if it is possible to draw a morally defensible distinction between these two nonpaternalistic restrictions of speech, then it is likewise possible to draw a morally defensible distinction between paternalistic restrictions. We can, for example, distinguish a paternalistic policy that prohibits swimming in lethal currents from a paternalistic policy that prohibits smoking marijuana as a form of medical treatment. We can do this on the ground that the reasons a person has to want to be prohibited from swimming in lethal currents have greater weight than the reasons a person has to want to be prohibited from smoking marijuana as a form of medical treatment, or on the ground that a person's reasons to want the freedom to smoke marijuana as a form of medical treatment have greater weight than the reasons anyone has to want to swim in lethal currents, or on both grounds. If these judgments about the relative weight of reasons are defensible, then it is perfectly coherent to hold that whereas unwanted paternalistic interference with the freedom to swim in lethal currents is justifiable, unwanted paternalistic interference with the freedom to use marijuana under medical supervision is not.

This shows how one may coherently hold that unwanted paternalistic heroin prohibition is justifiable without being committed in principle to the legitimacy of Kant's "paternal government." The justifiability of heroin prohibition, however, does not depend *solely* on the justifiability of any form of unwanted paternalism. This is because any policy that effectively prevents young people from self-destructive heroin use will also limit the liberty of mature adults in ways to which they have some reason to object. In order to be morally justifiable, the benefits of heroin prohibition to young people must therefore be great enough to justify this burden on *others*.

For reasons I have already given I think this judgment about the relative weight of benefits and burdens is correct, and that heroin prohibition is therefore morally justifiable in accordance with the individualistic principle of sufficient reason. Some may now object, though, that the individualistic principle of sufficient reason permits far too much government interference with our liberty.

This objection is similar to the standard line-drawing objection to the justifiability of unwanted paternalism but goes deeper in claiming that the individualistic principle of sufficient reason is inadequate as a basis on which to distinguish permissible from impermissible coercive government policies in general.

There are two ways in which this objection might be understood. On one interpretation, the objection is that a policy might violate someone's moral rights even if someone's reasons to want the government to adopt this policy have greater moral weight than anyone's reasons to want the government not to adopt it. To illustrate, suppose that the reasons of someone who struggles with obesity to want the government to prohibit the sale of fast-food burgers outweigh everyone else's reasons to want the freedom to buy and sell them. Does it follow that the government is morally permitted to prohibit their sale? Surely not, some will say. If they are right, then the individualistic principle of sufficient reason is invalid as a guide to what coercive government policies violate our moral rights.

In my view, this objection makes no sense. I think we can coherently believe that the government would violate someone's rights in prohibiting the sale of fast-food burgers only if we also believe that someone's reasons to want the freedom to buy or sell them have greater moral weight than anyone's reasons to want the government to prohibit their sale. If we believe to the contrary that someone's reasons to want the government to prohibit the sale of fast-food burgers have greater moral weight than everyone's reasons to want the government not to prohibit it, then, I think, we cannot coherently believe that this policy wrongs anyone and so cannot coherently believe that it violates anyone's moral rights.

There is, however, another way to understand the objection here to the individualistic principle of sufficient reason. This is that if the government were to adopt *all* the policies that the individualistic principle of sufficient reason permits, the cumulative impact on our liberty would be morally unacceptable. The objection here is similar to the standard objection to act utilitarianism that the cumulative impact of each person's acting in ways that maximize utility on subsequent occasions will be a net loss of utility. To illustrate, suppose that each person decides to burn wood in his fireplace by reasoning (correctly) in the following way: My burning wood in this fireplace tonight will give me great pleasure and will not itself cause anyone to suffer, so I should do it. If everyone reasons (correctly) like this on consecutive evenings and acts on this basis, the cumulative effect will be bad air for everyone, which will, over time, lower net utility by causing people to suffer. Might not a similar objection be made against the individualistic principle of sufficient reason, which is, in effect, a form of act individualism as applied to legislative acts?

Individual liberty has great value. Liberty is necessary for us to live in the ways best suited to our temperaments and abilities, and in ways that are most successful and satisfying. Liberty is necessary for us to have adequate control over the shape of our life, over the kind of life we lead, and over the kind of people we become. Liberty is a necessary social condition for the full development and exercise of our higher human capacities, such as the capacities for theoretical and practical reasoning. A system of liberty will be fully adequate only if it protects these and other important interests in liberty adequately, and any system of liberty that is not fully adequate in this sense will be morally objectionable. So if the individualistic principle of sufficient reason were to permit a set of policies that makes a fully adequate system of liberty impossible, I agree that it would be invalid.

If, however, the adoption of some policy by the government would make a system of liberty less than fully adequate, then someone would have a morally weighty reason to want the government to reject this policy, and, unless this policy were necessary to protect someone's fundamental rights, this reason would have at least as much moral weight as any reason someone had to want the government to adopt this policy, and the individualistic principle of sufficient reason would therefore not permit this policy. In some cases a policy will be incompatible with a fully adequate system of liberty only in tandem with some other liberty-limiting policy. In these cases, the reasons that someone has to want the government not to adopt both policies, or not to adopt the policy of adopting both, will have at least as much weight as the strongest reasons anyone has to want the government to adopt both, at least when having both policies is not necessary to protect anyone's fundamental rights, and the antecedent condition of the individualistic principle of sufficient reason will therefore not be satisfied. Which policy the government should adopt will then depend on the relative moral weight of individuals' reasons to want the relevant things from their government, but there is no reason to think that there will be sufficient reason for anyone to want the government to adopt *both* policies, if they are not both necessary to protect anyone's fundamental rights. For this reason I think it is false that the individualistic principle of sufficient reason permits too much government interference with our liberty.

I have now explained why I believe the familiar line-drawing objection is no more penetrating as directed against the individualistic principle of sufficient reason than it is as directed against the permissibility of unwanted paternalism. As directed against the policy of heroin prohibition, however, this objection might be made, not to discredit the individualistic principle of sufficient reason in general, but to discredit the claim that heroin prohibition satisfies this principle. Thus someone might argue as follows: None of us thinks the government would be justified in prohibiting the sale of fast-food burgers. So none of us believes that this policy satisfies the individualistic principle of sufficient reason. But the weightiest reason someone has to want heroin to be prohibited is no weightier than the weightiest reason someone has to want the sale of fast-food burgers to be prohibited, and the weightiest reason for someone to want heroin to be legal has at least as much weight as the weightiest reason anyone has to want the sale of fast-food burgers to be legal. So if we do not think that a policy of prohibiting the sale of fast-food burgers satisfies the individualistic principle of sufficient reason we cannot coherently think that a policy of heroin prohibition does either.

There is nothing wrong with the form of this argument. My objection is only to its content. I think it is not true that the weightiest reasons a person has to want heroin to be prohibited have no more weight than the weightiest reasons a person has to want the sale of fast-food burgers to be prohibited. The strongest reasons for people to want heroin to be prohibited, in my view, are grounded in their reasons to want certain opportunities that will play an important role in contributing to their overall life prospects to stay open. The strongest reasons for people to want the sale of fast-food burgers to be prohibited, on the other hand, are grounded in their reasons to want to live longer or in their reasons to want to be more physically attractive while they are alive. Although longevity and physical attractiveness are valuable, they are not, in my opinion, as important to one's ability to have a happy and successful life as adequate emotional development and education in childhood and adolescence. Furthermore, a failure to receive an adequate education in adolescence, along with the failure to develop emotionally as a result of heavy drug use, will typically have a lasting impact on the life of a person in a way that being overweight as a result of eating too many fast-food burgers at any particular point in one's life does not. This is partly because if one wishes to live longer or to look more attractive, one can decide to eat less now, and it is easier to eat less now – more within a person's voluntary control – than it is now to make up for the educational and other developmental opportunities one lost during adolescence. Moreover, because of the especially intense form of pleasure that heroin provides, I believe the ready availability of heroin will have a greater negative impact on the life of people than the ready availability of fast-food burgers does. Eating these burgers is pleasurable for some of us, to be sure, but they are not so uniquely or intensely pleasurable as heroin is for those who enjoy it. Finally, if fast-food restaurants are prohibited from selling burgers, other restaurants will still sell them, and one may still make them at home, and there are many other kinds of fatty food that can replace them. So the impact of fast-food burger prohibition on individual welfare will not in fact be so great. Of course, the government might prohibit the sale of *all* fatty foods, whether by restaurants or by supermarkets. This policy, however, would have a far greater negative impact on the quality of our life, our habits of socializing, our job opportunities, and the economy as a whole than the prohibition of heroin now does. The reasons for a person to want the sale of all fatty foods not to be prohibited therefore have greater weight than the strongest reasons anyone has to want heroin to be legalized. For these and other reasons I do not believe that the case for prohibiting the sale of fast-food burgers is as strong as the case for prohibiting heroin. Hence it does not follow, even loosely speaking, from the premise that fast-food burgers prohibition is morally unjustifiable that heroin prohibition is morally unjustifiable too.

If utilitarianism were the only moral theory to allow contingent empirical facts into our reasoning about what is right and wrong, this would be a powerful argument for it. The way in which the individualistic principle of sufficient reason allows empirical facts to bear on our moral reasoning within a nonaggregative, non-utilitarian, individualistic framework is thus something to be said in its favor. Observe, then, that this sensitivity to the facts blocks any simple reductio ad absurdum objection to heroin prohibition, such as the argument that if heroin prohibition is justifiable, then fast-food burger prohibition is justifiable too. Since the facts relevant to the assessment of any two policies will always be different, there will always be *some* basis on which to argue that one policy satisfies the individualistic principle of sufficient reason whereas the other one does not. There is thus no valid inference from the justifiability of one policy to the justifiability of another. Of course, in some cases, although the facts are quite different, the reasons for and against each policy will have exactly the same moral weight. If so, then if one policy is morally justifiable, the other is too. The point here is simply that since there are always potentially relevant distinctions between two different policies, one may not directly infer from the fact that one policy fails to satisfy the individualistic principle of sufficient reason that a completely different policy fails too. One must always argue *in addition* that the reasons for and against these two policies have exactly the same weight. Some may believe this to be true of the policies of heroin and fast-food burger prohibition. For the reasons just given, I do not.

8   Alcohol and Other Drugs

Alcohol Prohibition

I have now explained how it is perfectly coherent to defend heroin prohibition without also defending all sorts of other paternalistic policies such as the prohibition of fast-food burgers. Some may still wonder, though, whether it is possible coherently to defend heroin prohibition without also defending alcohol prohibition. Are not the independent harms of heavy drinking at least as great as the independent harms of heroin abuse? Might not these harms also be reduced substantially by a policy of prohibition? If so, does not alcohol prohibition satisfy the individualistic principle of sufficient reason at least as well as heroin prohibition does? If so, is not this an objection of sorts to the individualistic principle of reason as a test of whether a government policy violates our moral rights, since national Prohibition was such an obvious failure?

National Prohibition did fail politically,[1] but most scholars seem to agree that it succeeded in reducing per capita alcohol

---

[1] For some plausible hypotheses explaining this political failure, see Joseph R. Gusfield, *Symbolic Crusade: Status Politics and the American Temperance Movement* (Urbana: University of Illinois Press, 1963); J. C. Burnham, "New Perspectives on the Prohibition 'Experiment' of the 1920s," 2 *Journal of Social History* 51 (fall 1968); and Harry Gene Levine, "The Birth of American Alcohol Control: Prohibition, the Power Elite, and the Problem of Lawlessness," 12 *Contemporary Drug Problems* 63 (spring 1985).

consumption, and heavy drinking in particular.[2] An important piece of evidence is that the liver cirrhosis morality rate declined by nearly 50 percent during Prohibition, and admissions to state mental hospitals for alcoholic psychosis declined substantially as well. It is reasonable to believe, moreover, that if Prohibition had been effectively enforced and had retained solid political and cultural support over time, heavy drinking would have remained relatively low, with less damage to individuals as a result. This is supported by independent research that indicates that heavy drinking generally decreases with decreased availability and increased price, and that as heavy drinking decreases the independent harms of consumption generally decrease as well.[3]

What are these harms? Heavy drinking is positively associated with accidental death or injury, especially from automobiles, suicide, diseases such as cirrhosis, domestic and street violence, homicide and theft, sexual and other kinds of assault, and other serious harms, including emotional abuse and neglect within families.[4] Since there is a wide variation in the way heavy drinking

2 See, for example, Clark Warburton, *The Economic Results of Prohibition* (New York: Columbia University Press, 1932), p. 260; E. M. Jellinek, "Recent Trends in Alcoholism and in Alcohol Consumption," *Quarterly Journal of Studies on Alcohol* 8 (July 1947), pp. 9–10; Gusfield, *Symbolic Crusade*, pp. 118–19; Burnham, "New Perspectives," pp. 59–60; Norman H. Clark, *Deliver Us from Evil: An Interpretation of American Prohibition* (New York: Norton, 1976), pp. 146–7; Mark H. Moore, "Actually, Prohibition Was a Success," *The New York Times*, 16 October 1989, p. A21; Jeffrey A. Miron and Jeffrey Zweibel, "Alcohol Consumption during Prohibition," 81 *American Economic Review* 242 (May 1991); Griffith Edwards et al., *Alcohol Policy and the Public Good* (New York: Oxford University Press, 1994), p. 131; and Erich Goode, *Drugs in American Society*, 5th ed. (New York: McGraw-Hill, 1999), p. 186.

3 See Edwards et al., *Alcohol Policy and the Public Good*, pp. 119, 128, 141. They conclude (p. 205): "Generally, however, increase in per capita consumption will be followed by an increase in drinking across the drinking population, and an increase in the number of heavy drinkers, with consequences for rate of any particular problem depending on the curvature of the risk function" (emphasis deleted).

4 For the connection between alcohol abuse and crime and violence, see Jared R. Tinklenberg, "Alcohol and Violence," in Peter G. Bourne and Ruth Fox, eds., *Alcoholism: Progress in Research and Treatment* (New York: Academic Press, 1973); John A. O'Donnell et al., eds., *Young Men and Drugs – a Nationwide Survey*

affects behavior across cultures,[5] and even among individuals within the same culture, there is presumably no direct causal link between heavy drinking and harmful behavior. The positive association, however, between heavy drinking and crime and violence is so strong in our society as to indicate an indirect causal link. Whether this link is best explained by a pharmacological effect of depressing inhibitions, or of stimulating anger and aggressive impulses, or by the fact that, within our culture at least, heavy drinking is *expected* to have these psychological effects, is open to debate. What is not open to debate is that whatever the mechanism, heavy drinking seems to increase the risks of a wide array of antisocial and self-destructive conduct to a significant degree. If alcohol prohibition reduces these risks substantially, there is therefore a serious argument in its favor.

National Prohibition is commonly believed to have caused widespread violence and government corruption, but there was in fact no significant general increase of violent crime during the 1920s,[6] and it is not clear how much less corruption there would have been without Prohibition, given the general development of organized crime throughout the 1920s and its involvement in other illegal activities such as gambling and prostitution. Furthermore, it is arguable that increased police training and public accountability by elected officials, as well as the progressive weakening of organized crime in the last few decades, would reduce the corrupting impact of alcohol prohibition if it were adopted now.

(Rockville, MD: National Institute on Drug Abuse, 1976), pp. 83–4; Charles M. Evans, "Alcohol, Violence, and Aggression," 15 *British Journal on Alcohol and Alcoholism* 104 (1980); Vincent B. Van Hasselt, Randall L. Morrison, and Alan B. Bellack, "Alcohol Use in Wife Abusers and Their Spouses," 10 *Addictive Behaviors* 127 (1985); Phyllis Jo Baunach, "Jail Inmates 1983," *Bureau of Justice Statistics Bulletin* (November 1985), p. 7; Edwards et al., *Alcohol Policy and the Public Good*, pp. 53–67, 96–100; and Goode, *Drugs in American Society*, pp. 153–8.

5 See Craig MacAndrew and Robert B. Edgerton, *Drunken Comportment: A Social Explanation* (Chicago: Aldine, 1969).

6 See Edwin H. Sutherland and C. E. Gehlke, "Crime and Punishment," in *Recent Social Trends in the United States: Report of the President's Committee on Social Trends*, vol. 2 (New York: McGraw-Hill, 1933).

It is also important to bear in mind that alcohol prohibition proscribes only the manufacture and sale of alcoholic beverages. It does not prohibit drinking or making fermented or distilled beverages for personal use, and anyone can make an alcoholic beverage easily, by letting some cider sit unrefrigerated for a few days, for example. Furthermore, prohibition does not in fact prevent those with the money and inclination from buying higher-quality beverages on the black market. What prohibition does is make it more difficult and costly for everyone to acquire a high-quality beverage – to enjoy a fine wine with dinner, for example, or to have a top-shelf cocktail after work. This is a genuine burden. If, however, alcohol prohibition would reduce the independent harms of heavy drinking significantly, it is arguable that this burden on the recreational drinker is justifiable.

There are nonetheless important differences between the policies of heroin and alcohol prohibition that should stop us from concluding too quickly that they are equally defensible. For one thing, if my argument for heroin prohibition is sound, there are important differences in the risks to a person's life prospects posed by legalized heroin and legalized alcohol. My argument for heroin prohibition rests partly on the following assumptions: that because heroin is so intensely pleasurable, and because its use has a significant negative impact on motivation, and because social standards of normal use have not developed to control its use, the ready availability of safe and inexpensive heroin would result in many adolescents' using it regularly in a way that would cause them to ignore tasks they need to accomplish to prepare adequately for a successful, independent adulthood. Alcohol, in contrast, although it is certainly pleasurable for those who enjoy it, is not so intensely pleasurable as heroin; nor does its negative impact on motivation generally seem so strong. Furthermore, norms for alcohol use have developed, even among teenagers. Thus although it seems to us relatively normal for teenagers to get drunk on illicit alcohol at parties on weekends, it seems relatively abnormal for them to drink during school hours or even after school on schooldays. Without a system of norms governing its use, the easy availability of heroin is thus likely to have a worse impact on the participation of young people in school and other activities.

Another important difference between heroin prohibition and alcohol prohibition is that adopting a policy of alcohol prohibition now would impose a serious burden on individuals who work in the alcoholic beverage industry. A person whose life revolves around operating a bar or around making wine or beer for sale will lose a great deal if his or her occupation or way of life is suddenly made illegal. This objection might be overcome if the government were to make a serious commitment to retraining workers and to making other business options available by extending credit. Still, this burden constitutes an important objection to alcohol prohibition that does not exist to heroin prohibition, since those who have decided to make their living dealing heroin have done so with full knowledge that it is illegal.

The most important difference, though, between alcohol prohibition and heroin prohibition is that because drinking is far more socially accepted and far more deeply woven into the fabric of normal social interaction than heroin use is, one may reasonably believe that alcohol prohibition now will not be nearly as effective in reducing the independent harms of alcohol abuse as heroin prohibition is in reducing the independent harms of heroin abuse. The present policy of heroin prohibition is supported by a general, arguably mistaken belief that heroin use is both morally wrong and extremely dangerous in itself, and by the widespread belief that no healthy person, if fully rational, would want to use heroin recreationally given its dangers. Many regard drinking, by contrast, as perfectly normal and benign. A legal prohibition enforced against a form of conduct that the majority regards as normal and harmless is far less likely to be effective than one enforced against a form of conduct of which the majority strongly disapproves. So even if the independent harms of heavy drinking are worse than those of heavy heroin use, it does not directly follow that alcohol prohibition is justifiable, since it may be far less effective in reducing these harms, given the general social acceptance of drinking.

Although these important differences do exist between the two policies, however, the negative impact on individuals' lives of alcohol abuse is nonetheless quite substantial. So if heroin prohibition can be justified by the kind of argument that I have given, arguably alcohol prohibition is justifiable too. To be sure, a policy of alcohol prohibition now would negatively impact many more people than heroin prohibition does because so many more people enjoy drinking than wish to use heroin. But if what I said in the previous chapter about rights and justification is correct, then the mere fact that a policy burdens more people than it benefits is not a decisive argument against it. It may still be justifiable if the reasons for someone to prefer his or her situation under this policy have greater weight than the reasons of anyone to prefer his or her situation without it.

Although there is no valid inference, then, from the justifiability of heroin prohibition to the justifiability of alcohol prohibition, it is possible that a persuasive case for alcohol prohibition might be made given the view of rights taken here. Some may take this to constitute an objection to this approach to rights, but, not surprisingly, I do not. To the contrary, if alcohol prohibition were justifiable in accordance with the individualistic principle of sufficient reason, then, in my view, this policy would *not* violate anyone's moral rights.

We are not, of course, likely to return to a policy of national prohibition any time soon, but the in-principle justifiability of alcohol prohibition is relevant to our current thinking about drug policy in two ways. First, if alcohol prohibition is justifiable in principle, then an argument for drug prohibition that suggests this is not open to objection on this ground. Second, if alcohol prohibition is justifiable in principle, then other policies that restrict our freedom to drink, which are already in place or are more likely to be adopted in the future, may also be morally justifiable.

Consider in this connection the policy of the Navajo to prohibit the sale of alcohol on the reservation. Or consider the policy of some towns to prohibit the sale of liquor within town limits, or of states and towns to permit the sale of liquor only at certain

locations or during certain times. If these policies function to reduce violence, crime, and self-destructive drinking, they might
well be justified as compatible with the individualistic principle
of sufficient reason, and so they might be adopted without violating anyone's moral rights. We can agree, if we like, that individuals have a general right to liberty that covers the freedom
to drink. All this general right prohibits, however, are coercive
government policies that limit individual liberty for insufficient
reason. If, then, the individualistic principle of sufficient reason
is valid, and a policy of alcohol control satisfies this principle, this
policy violates no one's moral rights.

Marijuana, Cocaine, LSD

I have now defended heroin prohibition and allowed that alcohol
prohibition might also be justified on certain assumptions. What,
then, about other drugs? Is the prohibition of marijuana, cocaine (including crack), speed (methamphetamine), psychedelics
such as LSD, ecstasy (MDMA), barbiturates, or cigarettes, likewise
justifiable?

If any of these drugs is as pleasurable and motivationally enervating as heroin appears to be, then there is an argument for
prohibiting this drug that is of equal weight to the argument for
prohibiting heroin. If any of these drugs causes violence and other
forms of antisocial conduct to the same extent heavy drinking
seems to, then there is an argument for prohibiting this drug that
is of equal weight to the argument for prohibiting alcohol. If the
prohibition of this other drug would then substantially reduce
the independent harms that would result from its abuse, with a
gradual and proportionate system of penalties, then the case for
prohibiting it is at least as strong as the case is for prohibiting
heroin or alcohol.

Suppose, though, that no other drug *is* as motivationally enervating as heroin and that no other drug *does* cause violence and
other forms of antisocial conduct to the degree that alcohol does,
as seems to be the case. How strong *then* is the case for prohibiting
these other drugs?

The most widely used illegal drug is marijuana. Studies indicate that about a third of Americans older than 12 years old have tried this drug; that about 1 in 10 has used it within the past year; and that 1 in 17 has used it in the past month.[7] No doubt partly because of its relative social acceptability, a number of states have legalized its possession. I myself would advocate removing substantial criminal penalties for the possession of small quantities of marijuana everywhere for reasons already suggested in the previous chapters. Is there nonetheless a good argument for prohibiting the manufacture and sale of marijuana or for making possession a misdemeanor?

Not surprisingly, the argument against marijuana legalization that I would find most compelling, if true, is that this policy would result in more marijuana use among middle and high school students and that this would have the effect of depressing academic performance and so of weakening a young person's preparation for adulthood. Although there is reason to doubt that marijuana causes the kind of "amotivational syndrome" that I have associated with heroin,[8] there is also some reason to believe that heavy use does interfere with optimal intellectual development and performance,[9] and that is an argument against legalization.

Another common argument against marijuana legalization is that its use is a "gateway" to use of other drugs. The thought here is that marijuana use "opens the door" to the use of "harder" drugs, particularly heroin and cocaine, and so makes their use more likely. The evidence for this is a strong statistical correlation between marijuana use and the later use of cocaine and heroin.[10] That is, although many people have never used marijuana, very few of those who have used heroin or cocaine did not use

---

7 Goode, *Drugs in American Society*, p. 127.

8 Ibid., pp. 232–4.

9 Goode concludes that marijuana is "highly likely to impair thinking, learning, and memory, as well as other crucial cognitive processes," *Drugs in American Society*, p. 221.

10 See Lee N. Robins, "The Natural History of Drug Abuse," in Dan J. Lettieri et al., eds., *Theories on Drug Abuse* (Rockville, MD: National Institute on Drug Abuse, 1980), p. 222; and Goode, *Drugs in American Society*, p. 228.

marijuana first. There is, however, considerable doubt about whether there is any genuine causal connection here.[11] It is quite possible that a person who is psychologically disposed to seek the recreational enjoyment of marijuana is also disposed to seek the recreational enjoyment of heroin but is more likely to use marijuana first simply because it is more easily available and less socially stigmatized. Furthermore, some explanations of the correlation between marijuana use and later heroin use seem to warrant legalization rather than prohibition. So suppose the best explanation for the statistical correlation between marijuana use and later heroin use is that those teenagers who become accustomed to breaking the law by smoking marijuana, which is more easily available and less socially stigmatized, are then more willing to break the law in order to use heroin. If this is the best explanation, then the legalization of marijuana would presumably weaken the role of marijuana as a gateway drug, and the gateway effect could not be coherently cited as a reason for prohibition.

Suppose, though, for the sake of argument, that marijuana use would increase the likelihood of heroin use even if marijuana were legal. One possible explanation for this is that a person who has become high on marijuana and who has enjoyed this experience is more likely to search for an even more intense high somewhere else than someone who has never gotten high. This gateway effect would then provide an argument for marijuana prohibition that is related to the one I have given for heroin prohibition if the resulting heroin use were to occur relatively early in a person's life. Suppose, for example, that if marijuana were legalized, many more 13-year-olds would smoke it regularly than do now, and that a significant percentage of them who would not otherwise have done so would start using heroin regularly three years later, thus significantly raising the number of adolescents who use heroin with bad consequences for their education,

11 For a recent rigorous examination of the gateway hypothesis, see Denise B. Kandel, ed., *Stages and Pathways of Drug Involvement: Examining the Gateway Hypothesis* (Cambridge: Cambridge University Press, 2002). Kandel concludes (p. 366): "At this time, the causal interpretation of the Gateway Hypothesis is still without scientific foundation."

emotional development, and life prospects. This would be a reason to prohibit marijuana that was independent of its own negative impact on motivation. So the gateway effect, if genuine, would provide another important argument for marijuana prohibition.

A serious obstacle remains, though, to justifying marijuana prohibition in either of these ways, which is that because marijuana is so widely used and is so socially accepted, relatively speaking, this policy is less likely to reduce the relevant risks of marijuana use substantially. In the previous section I observed that the main difference between the justifiability of heroin prohibition and that of alcohol prohibition is the difference in social attitudes toward these drugs. In this respect, marijuana is arguably closer to alcohol than it is to heroin. If so, then, even if the greater availability of marijuana would increase the risks of self-destructive drug abuse to some adolescents, the amount by which prohibition can be expected to reduce this risk might not be great enough to justify the burdens of criminal liability that this policy would impose.

Personally I doubt that greater availability of marijuana would substantially increase the risk to teenagers of failing to develop emotionally or of doing poorly in school. This is partly because marijuana is not so intensely pleasurable and motivationally enervating as heroin is, and partly because I am skeptical of the gateway hypothesis. Furthermore, I suspect that marijuana prohibition is relatively ineffective because marijuana use is socially accepted. Taken together, these considerations suggest to me that the benefits of prohibition are too low to justify its costs, and for this reason I am inclined to support not only marijuana decriminalization, but marijuana legalization as well.

One familiar argument for heroin prohibition that I have not paid any attention to is that heroin use causes crime.[12] I have ignored this argument since I believe, with many others, that,

12 Robert J. MacCoun and Peter Reuter, *Drug War Heresies: Learning from Other Vices, Times, and Places* (Cambridge: Cambridge University Press, 2002), p. 276: "In all nations for which information is available, studies show high crime rates among frequent users of heroin."

since legalization would make heroin more affordable, it would remove a major incentive to property crime, and that therefore one can reasonably believe that crime rates would be reduced by heroin legalization. The connection between property crime and heroin use is not quite so simple as this conjecture suggests, however, since those who choose a life of heroin use will be less willing to work for a living and so will be more motivated to support themselves by crime. For this reason it is *possible* that crime rates would go up if heroin were legalized. How weighty an argument this is for prohibition depends on the amount by which crime rates are likely to increase, a figure that is very difficult to state with any confidence.

Though crime prevention is not the main argument I have given for heroin prohibition, it is part of the main argument I have considered for alcohol prohibition, and alcohol is not the only drug whose heavy use is strongly correlated with crime; so is the heavy use of stimulants such as cocaine and speed.[13] Does crime prevention, then, also justify the prohibition of these drugs?

This depends on what factors best explain the correlation. One part of the explanation is that those who are willing to break the law in order to use these drugs are also more likely to break other laws. Another part of the explanation is that the culture surrounding buying and selling drugs on the street is more violent and less effectively regulated by norms of civility than other activities. But cocaine and speed, and other street drugs, such as "angel dust" (PCP), may also depress inhibitions or stimulate aggressive behavior in the way that alcohol seems to. If they do, this would be an independent argument for their prohibition. Furthermore, even if the use of these drugs does not raise the risks of crime by as much as heavy drinking does, their prohibition might nonetheless be more justifiable than alcohol prohibition, since the use of these drugs is not so deeply woven into the fabric of normal socializing in our society, and so their prohibition is more likely to be effective.

13 See Goode, *Drugs in American Society*, pp. 160–2.

Another common argument for prohibiting cocaine and speed is that, because these drugs are so intensely pleasurable for those who enjoy them, people who enjoy them commonly become obsessed with their use, which then becomes the focus of their daily pursuits, and this obsession has a destructive impact on the user's life and on the life of those around him or her. Here it is arguable, though, that the heavy use of these drugs is destructive in this way primarily because they are illegal. Because they are illegal, acquiring them takes energy and costs a lot of money and using them can result in being arrested or fired from one's job. What we must assess in evaluating prohibition is how harmful the heavy use of these drugs would be *if they were legal*. If these drugs were legal, it is likely that more people would act edgy and emotionally disconnected as a result of using them. This would certainly be a disadvantage for family members, coworkers, and others who must interact with them. It is doubtful, though, that this emotional effect *alone* could justify criminal penalties.

For this reason, I think the central question in evaluating the prohibition of cocaine and speed is the degree to which the heavy use of these drugs increases violence and other kinds of interpersonal abuse. Although it is certainly arguable that the negative effect of these drugs is not so bad as the negative effects of alcohol, it also possible that the greater use of these drugs *together with* alcohol would increase the independent harms of drug and alcohol abuse substantially. When people use speed or cocaine, they are able to drink more and drink longer. Whatever negative effects heavy drinking generally has – depressed inhibition, aroused aggression, poor judgment, peculiar behavior – are therefore likely to be intensified if people use these other drugs more heavily. If a policy prohibition were to function, then, to reduce the heavy use of these drugs substantially, I think their prohibition might be justified on this ground.

An influential argument for legalizing heroin is that it would make heroin safer to use for addicts and others and so would reduce the risk of fatal overdose. As I observed in the previous chapter, however, heroin legalization would also result in more people's using heroin and so would increase the risk of fatal overdose to some people. It might also raise the risk of death through suicide, since death by heroin overdose is a relatively attractive means of killing oneself. These risks seem to me great enough to offset the increased risk of overdose created by prohibition, and so to nullify this argument for legalization.

Related points might now be made about barbiturates, which, especially when mixed with alcohol, can also be quite lethal. Because of their mental health benefits, barbiturates are not prohibited; rather their sale is strictly regulated to reduce the risks of both accidental and intentional overdose. But it is natural to wonder here whether the mental health benefits of potentially lethal barbiturates are really any greater than the potential mental health benefits of heroin. If not, and the only reason to prohibit heroin were the health risks legalization would create, then it would seem that the law should treat them in the same way: It should either prohibit both or legalize both and regulate them.

The health risks that would be created by legalizing heroin do not, however, provide the strongest argument for prohibition, in my opinion. The primary risks of legalization concern instead the predictable impact of heroin abuse on motivation. Furthermore, both the motivational risks and the health risks would be intensified by the intense pleasure heroin provides to those who enjoy it. Since barbiturates are not so intensely pleasurable, the case for prohibiting barbiturates is therefore weaker. For these reasons it is perfectly consistent to hold that although heroin prohibition can be justified, strict regulation is the strongest policy that can be justified with respect to barbiturates.

One argument for heroin prohibition that I have rejected outright is that drug use is simply wrong or bad in itself, or that a person mistreats his own mind and so himself by taking drugs for the purpose of altering his states of consciousness. I believe there is nothing inherently wrong with a person's altering his states of consciousness for the purposes of relaxation, enjoyment, or self-exploration, and so nothing wrong in itself with one person's selling a drug to another person for these purposes. If not, then it is hard to state any good argument for prohibiting the psychedelic drugs – LSD, mescaline, peyote, mushrooms – or the euphoric/empathic drug ecstasy. Despite anecdotal reports of permanent psychological and physical damage, careful research suggests that these drugs are relatively benign.[14] It is virtually impossible to overdose on them; they do not lead to violence or other kinds of crime; they are unlikely to undermine motivation; and they seem to have greater psychological benefits than many other drugs, in terms of offering a fresh perspective on life or in intensifying warm and benevolent feelings toward others, at least while one is under their influence. Although these drugs might be regulated, then, to discourage use that is psychologically disturbing, I think that the case for prohibition is very weak.

Cigarette smoking raises different issues from any of the drugs I have considered so far. Smoking does not undermine motivation. It does not increase people's aggressiveness or remove their inhibitions. It does not present a threat of fatal overdose. The reasons to prohibit cigarette smoking are therefore far less like the reasons to prohibit the manufacture and sale of currently illegal drugs than they are like the reasons to prohibit the manufacture and sale of fatty foods. Whether cigarette-smoking prohibition is justifiable, and if so, to what extent, is therefore a different kind of issue from the prohibition of currently illegal drugs.

This serves to emphasize the important point made at the end of the previous chapter that to endorse the prohibition of one activity or substance is not to endorse the prohibition of any other. Coherence does not require someone who believes that heroin prohibition is justifiable on the grounds I have given also to believe that the prohibition of any other drug is justifiable, or that the prohibition of cigarette smoking is justifiable, or that the prohibition of fast-food burgers is justifiable. If other drugs are connected with a self-destructive loss of motivation in the way heroin is, or with violence and other forms of antisocial conduct the way alcohol is, then the argument for prohibiting these other drugs might be at least as strong. Whether this is true, however, depends upon the empirical facts. Since it is quite possible that no drug is

14 Ibid., pp. 260–2.

as damaging as heroin or alcohol, it is open to someone to hold that these forms of prohibition are justifiable without believing that others are.

The Value of Individuality

One of the main arguments against paternalism that Mill offers in *On Liberty* is that paternalistic policies stifle human development by stifling human individuality, which he understands to consist in uniqueness in personality or way of life.[15] Mill values individuality both as an essential constituent of full human development and as a means to the full development and exercise of other important higher human capacities, such as the capacities for theoretical and practical reason, aesthetic judgment and discrimination, and love and friendship. Mill suggests that paternalistic policies stifle human individuality and so retard human development by imposing the moral prejudices of a narrow-minded moral majority on an unconventional minority. For this reason, he maintains, individuality and human development would be best promoted over time by the observance by society of a general principle of antipaternalism.

Rule-consequentialist arguments of this kind are open to standard objections when they are offered to justify exceptionless rules of the kind Mill apparently aims to defend in *On Liberty*. To illustrate, suppose there is one form of unwanted paternalism that promotes individuality or human development more generally – seat-belt laws, for example, which promote individuality indirectly because one cannot develop individuality unless one is alive. The principle of antipaternalism can now be reformulated to allow this particular form of paternalism, and individuality and human development will now be better promoted by observing *this* principle, which allows this one exception, than by observing an exceptionless principle that prohibits all forms of unwanted paternalism.

15 See J. S. Mill, *On Liberty*, ed. Elizabeth Rapaport (Indianapolis: Hackett, 1978), pp. 53–71.

This general point, however, about rule-consequentialist methods of justification does not crush Mill's individuality argument against paternalism. This is because it is still arguable that the paternalistic policies that Mill was most concerned to reject *do* stifle individuality, and so human development, and that they are unjustifiable for this reason. Indeed, one might think this is true of drug prohibition. So I should say something in response to this argument.

The only policy of drug prohibition that I have fully endorsed here is the prohibition of heroin. I have now allowed, however, that a good case might also be made for prohibiting alcohol, and cocaine and speed. So I want to consider the following set of policies for the sake of illustration: Heroin, alcohol, cocaine, and speed are prohibited, but marijuana, barbiturates, the psychedelics, and ecstasy are only regulated. Is there any reason to worry that this set of policies would threaten our individuality, or human development more generally, over time?

The paternalistic argument I have given for heroin prohibition presupposes that the heavy use of heroin during adolescence will *thwart* the development and exercise of the higher human capacities, including the capacity for individuality. So, in my view, a policy of prohibition that is adopted for the sake of those who would abuse it is *supported* by the value of human development. But heroin prohibition also discourages some adolescents and adults who would not abuse it from using heroin, and it is arguable that prohibition thus stifles *their* individuality and development. Perhaps, then, this loss of individuality to them outweighs the benefits of prohibition to those at greater risk of self-destructive heroin abuse.

Studies do suggest that adolescents who are willing to use illegal drugs are typically less conventional and less conformist, more willing to challenge authority and challenge conventional beliefs and attitudes.[16] Those adolescents who are willing to use illegal drugs will thus typically exemplify a higher degree of individuality

16 Richard Jessor and Shirley Jessor, "A Social Psychological Framework for Studying Drug Abuse," in Dan J. Lettieri et al., eds., *Theories on Drug Abuse*, p. 109; Denise B. Kandel, "Marijuana Users in Young Adulthood," 41 *Archives of General Psychiatry* 204 (February 1984).

than those who are not. There is, however, no reason to believe that drug use *promotes* this kind of individuality rather than the other way around. Timothy Leary was surely a nonconformist before he ever took LSD and would certainly have remained one if he never had. Furthermore, drugs such as LSD that arguably do most to promote individuality are not the ones whose prohibition is at stake here.

Some may think heroin use promotes individuality because many innovative young jazz musicians have used it over the years. Not to my knowledge, though, has any major figure claimed that heroin enhanced his musicianship or advanced his career. If anything, the opposite seems to be true.[17] Moreover, it is far more probable that heroin use by talented young musicians results from the unconventional outlook and emotional intensity that enable them to be innovative performers in the first place, combined with the life and environment of a career in music, than it is that their musical originality results from their heroin use, which seems typically to begin only after they have established themselves as professional musicians.

In support of the contention that drug use promotes individuality, some may point to the way in which marijuana seems to have inspired original popular music in the 1960s and 1970s and the worldviews associated with this music. It seems to have inspired music by the Beatles and Bob Marley, for example, and to have promoted the associated messages of peace and love. The fact, however, that marijuana was illegal in Britain, Jamaica, and the United States when these musical forms and associated worldviews developed casts doubt onto the claim that *prohibition* undermines individuality. Indeed, it is arguable that marijuana played an important cultural role in the 1960s and 1970s largely *because* it was illegal and so its use expressed a rejection of certain conventions and certain kinds of authority.[18] Moreover, given

17 For entertaining anecdotal support, see Miles Davis, *Miles* (New York: Simon & Schuster, 1989).

18 Edward M. Brecher, *Licit and Illicit Drugs* (Mt. Vernon, NY: Consumers Union, 1972), pp. 494–8, attributes the increase of drug use by youth during the 1960s partly to rising concern among parents and other authority figures about the dangers of drug use.

the widespread use of marijuana among artists and musicians in places where it is now still illegal, whether legalizing marijuana would result in any *further* musical or cultural achievements is open to doubt. So our cultural experience with marijuana provides little support to the general claim that drug prohibition stifles individuality.

What, then, about prohibiting alcohol, cocaine, and speed? In defending the value of individuality, Mill did not argue that any policy that limits individuality is unjustifiable, since he allowed that actions that harm others may be prohibited even if these actions enhance or promote someone's individuality. For reasons that are obscure, Mill apparently assumed in *On Liberty* that alcohol prohibition is a paternalistic policy[19] and so is an unjustifiable intrusion upon individuality. But on the analysis I proposed in the previous chapter, a policy is genuinely paternalistic only if it cannot be fully justified by nonpaternalistic reasons alone, and alcohol prohibition seemingly *can* be justified by nonpaternalistic reasons, if it can be justified at all, since the strongest argument in its favor is to reduce a person's risk of unwanted injury from *others* who are drinking. Likewise with cocaine and speed. If, then, the case for the prohibition of these drugs is sound, the fact that it limits individuality to *some* degree should not be regarded as a decisive reason against it, even from Mill's point of view.

There is, in any case, no reason to believe that these forms of prohibition would stifle individuality or human development overall. To be sure, alcohol prohibition would make certain colorful characters like the salty bartender or the disintegrating barfly less common than they now are, and these characters may display a certain kind of individuality. Individuality, however, has its greatest weight as a reason against government interference only when it functions to advance the development and exercise of *other* higher human capacities in important ways, and these character types and associated ways of life seem not to have great instrumental value of this kind. Given, then, the negative impact that heavy drinking typically has on the development and

19 Mill, *On Liberty*, pp. 99–100.

exercise of the higher human capacities, there is little reason to believe that this policy will result in a *net loss* in human development. And similar points may be made about the prohibition of cocaine and methamphetamine. Although the prohibition of these drugs may decrease the frequency of a certain kind of nervous and self-absorbed personality, this is unlikely to represent a net loss in terms of human development. So if an increase in the use of these drugs would result in an increase in violence and other forms of antisocial conduct, there is little reason to object to their prohibition on grounds of individuality.

9   Epistemic Concerns

I N stating an argument for heroin prohibition, and in considering the justifiability of other forms of drug control, I have made
a number of empirical assumptions that may fairly be questioned.
Indeed all my key empirical assumptions might be false, and even
if they are true, it is natural to wonder whether we are actually
justified in believing them. This is ultimately a matter for social
science to determine. But some may wonder, how much evidence
must we have in general, and what kind of evidence, to be justified in supporting coercive government policies of this kind?

Coercive government policies can be justified in general only
by good reasons, and good reasons are constituted only by true
propositions. A person is justified in believing a proposition true
when the information available to her provides her with good
epistemic reasons to believe it and these reasons outweigh the
good epistemic reasons to doubt it that are also provided by the
information available to her. Being justified, however, in believing a proposition that supports a policy does not suffice to justify one in supporting it. One must also be justified in believing
that the reasons in support of this policy outweigh the reasons
against it. In my opinion, one is justified in believing a judgment
of this kind when it withstands one's critical scrutiny: when this
judgment about the relative weight of reasons continues to seem
correct over time and to cohere with the other judgments one
makes about the relative weight of reasons. Suppose, then, that
a person is justified in believing a proposition and is also justified
in believing that this proposition constitutes a reason in favor of

a coercive policy that has greater weight than any reason against it. Does this suffice to justify this person in supporting this policy? We typically think that the more burdensome a coercive policy is, the stronger the epistemic case must be in favor of believing the propositions that count in favor of this policy. If a policy is very burdensome, then the epistemic grounds for believing at least one of the propositions that provide a sufficient reason for this policy must be very strong. If a policy is not so burdensome, then these epistemic grounds need not be so strong. I accept this commonsense view.

How, then, does this general approach to justification bear on drug prohibition? The freedom to buy and sell certain drugs such as heroin, although it is certainly valuable, is not so valuable that its limitation imposes the heaviest of burdens, since this policy leaves open many other opportunities for employment and enjoyment (including, as a matter of fact, illegal opportunities). So, if we accept the general view of justification just sketched, then, although we do need to be justified in believing the empirical assumptions of any argument for drug prohibition, we need not be justified in feeling *absolutely certain* about them in order to be justified in supporting this policy. Our reasons for believing these propositions need only be stronger than our reasons to doubt them.

My argument for heroin prohibition is based on three key empirical assumptions: first, that heroin legalization will result in a substantial increase in heroin abuse; second, that heroin abuse will commonly undermine a person's motivation to accomplish certain important tasks, such as caring for one's children and completing one's education, which will result in some people's having substantially worse life prospects; third, that heroin abuse can be substantially reduced by a policy of prohibition even when this policy is enforced by a gradual and proportionate system of penalties. Is there sufficient reason, then, to accept these assumptions?

It is an axiom of enlightened public policy that no criminal penalty is justified unless it deters conduct that is harmful or unfair in some way. The justification for any criminal law thus presupposes that it has some deterrent effect. This is no less true of laws prohibiting murder than it is of laws prohibiting the manufacture and sale of drugs. We have no direct empirical evidence, however, that murder is deterred by criminal laws. It is possible that murder rates would stay flat or even decline if murder were legalized. We are justified in believing the contrary on the basis of general assumptions about human rationality. We know that it will seem to someone to be to his advantage in some way or another to murder someone else and that he will therefore be motivated to do so unless the probable bad consequences of doing so are serious enough to make the risks seem worse than the likely benefits. On this basis we conclude that the threat of prosecution, conviction, and imprisonment functions to deter some people from murder. If, however, we are justified in believing that murder laws deter on this general basis, we are also justified in believing that laws prohibiting the manufacture and sale of drugs will deter people from manufacturing and selling them.

If people are deterred from manufacturing and selling drugs by the risk of criminal liability, then fewer drugs will be manufactured and sold, and drugs will therefore be less readily available. There is some empirical evidence, then, to support the belief that drug use and abuse decrease with availability. One piece of evidence is the fact that alcohol consumption declined during national Prohibition.[1] Another piece of evidence is that although almost half of U.S. enlisted men used heroin or opium in Vietnam, where it was easily available, only about one-fifth of those who had used heroin or opium in Vietnam continued to use it back in the United States, where it was much less available.[2] Another piece of evidence is that the illegal use of narcotics is much higher than one would expect among medical professionals, who have easier access to them.[3] How do we know, then, that drug *abuse* would increase with use? This claim is supported by studies that

1 See Chapter 7, footnote 2.
2 See Lee N. Robins, "Drug Use by U.S. Army in Vietnam: A Follow-up on Their Return Home," 99 *American Journal of Epidemiology* 235 (1974).
3 See Erich Goode, *Drugs in American Society*, 5th ed. (New York: McGraw-Hill, 1999), pp. 402–4.

indicate that this is true of drinking.[4] Taking all these considerations together, I believe there is sufficient reason to accept my
first assumption, that heroin legalization will result in a substantial increase in heroin abuse.

It is harder to find specific empirical support for my second key
assumption, which is that an increase in heroin use would lead
to the kind of debilitating abuse that I fear. Even if heroin abuse
would be relatively common among neglectful parents and un-
motivated teenagers once legalized, that the drug abuse *causes*
these states does not follow. Perhaps it works the other way
around: that whatever inclines a person to neglect her children
or to avoid doing well in high school also leads a person to abuse
drugs. Perhaps, in other words, drug abuse is nothing but a symptom of an underlying pathological state and never a contributing
cause. I believe to the contrary that although drug abuse is typically a symptom of other psychological difficulties, drug abuse
itself exacerbates these difficulties and so creates further difficulties that are independent of drug illegality. Although it is hard to
find empirical confirmation for this, it fits well enough with what
we know.

In reaching my own conclusion about the dangers of heroin
abuse, I have admittedly relied on anecdotal reports of people's
experience with heroin. Consider for example this report of her
experience with heroin by a white Jewish woman in a middle-
class family, which is taken from a leading (nonpolemical) text-
book on drugs:

> I knew a lot of people who got high with me who had a lot of
> potential and their lives were ruined by dope. They're never
> going to get anywhere. I'm 29 years old. I wish that, by now,
> my career was all settled for me. That I had friends. You don't
> know how to be a friend or what a relationship is when you're
> just getting high. And when you stop getting high, it's like being
> a baby and starting all over again from the beginning. . . . The
> main thing that bothers me is that the years that I lost while

4 See Griffith Edwards et al., *Alcohol Policy and the Public Good* (New York: Oxford
University Press, 1994), p. 205.

I was taking dope I will never get back. And you lose a lot of self-pride because of the things you end up doing, and it takes a long time to get that back. What I should have been doing all that time in my life was going to college, pursuing a career, and going out and doing the so-called normal things. What I was doing was hanging out on the street corner and getting high. And that was my whole life. . . . If I hadn't gotten involved in drugs maybe I would have had a career. Maybe I would have had more confidence in myself at this point in my life. . . . Maybe I would have been married.[5]

Heroin did not *destroy* this person, and she goes on to say that she is now able to function better in the world. Her story, however, leaves one with a strong sense of permanent loss. I believe that if heroin were legalized stories like this one would be much more common, and that legalization would have an especially negative impact on young people with fewer advantages starting out than this woman had.

Whether stories of this kind provide an adequate basis for policy is certainly open to question. But it is important to point out that many of our policies must be based on commonsense conjectures about the harmful psychological effects of legalizing some activity that are not open to direct empirical confirmation, especially some of those that bear on the welfare of young people. Consider, for example, laws against statutory rape, which prohibit adults from having sexual relations with children and teenagers. The only plausible justification for this policy, it seems to me, is that (even unforced) sexual relations between adults and minors are likely to harm the minors psychologically in ways that they do not yet understand and cannot predict and that this law functions to deter this conduct. It is *possible* that sex between adults and minors is not generally harmful, and that the law does not, in any case, do anything to deter it. Perhaps the only minors who now seem to be harmed by sex with adults are those who were already emotionally troubled in some way and so would in any case later have had the emotional problems that seem to be

5 Goode, *Drugs in American Society*, pp. 344–5.

associated with sexual abuse. If we are justified in believing the contrary, it is only on the basis of anecdote and general beliefs about human psychology, and general assumptions about the efficacy of the law to deter conduct. If, then, someone challenges the argument I have given for heroin laws on the grounds that we are not justified in believing that heroin abuse commonly has the bad effects I have supposed, I suggest that the same is probably true of many other laws, including some that are far less controversial. Of course one might challenge my analogy here by arguing that adult sex with minors should be prohibited even if it is not psychologically harmful just because it is immoral. But this argument is no better, in my view, than the argument for drug criminalization, which I reject, that drug use should be prohibited just because it is immoral.

What, then, of my third key assumption, that drug prohibition will reduce drug use even when enforced by a gradual and proportionate system of penalties? The best way to test this hypothesis is to try it out. Since drug prohibition will be justifiable in any case only with a gradual and proportionate system of penalties, aiming now at making the penalties gradual and proportionate and seeing what happens make sense.

One of the main arguments I have given for prohibiting heroin is paternalistic, and some have argued that the justification of paternalistic policies presents special epistemic problems. Thus Mill suggests in *On Liberty* that unwanted paternalism is impermissible because a legislator is never justified in believing that another mature adult is mistaken about what is best for her.[6] When two people, Jones and Smith, disagree about whether a policy that limits Smith's liberty is in Smith's best interest, Jones is not justified in believing that this policy is in Smith's best interest, because Smith knows her own situation better and cares more about her own welfare than Jones does, and therefore "the odds are," as Mill puts it, that Jones is wrong in his belief that the policy will benefit Smith. Jones is therefore not justified in believing that

6 See J. S. Mill, *On Liberty*, ed. Elizabeth Rapaport (Indianapolis: Hackett, 1978), pp. 74, 81.

Smith will be benefited by a policy that limits her liberty against her will and so is not justified in supporting an unwanted law for this reason.

Significantly, Mill limits this claim to apply only to those who are "in the maturity of their faculties."[7] He thus evidently believed that if Smith is not in the maturity of her faculties, then Jones might be justified in believing that Smith is wrong about what is best for her. On the assumption, then, that adolescents and young adults are not in the maturity of their faculties, Mill's epistemic argument does not apply to the policy of heroin prohibition that I have defended here.

Suppose, though, for the sake of argument, that young adults are in the maturity of their faculties in the sense relevant to the moral assessment of paternalistic heroin prohibition. We might still wonder whether there is any compelling reason to agree with Mill's suggestion that no legislator can be justified in believing that someone who is in the maturity of her faculties is wrong about what is best for her. Mill was no doubt right to suggest that if a fully mature person who is sane and adequately informed believes that it is in her best interest to do something, this is a good reason for a legislator to doubt that a policy that prohibits her from doing this thing is actually in her best interest. But Mill gives no good reason to believe that this doubt cannot reasonably be overcome. Although it is surely true in general that a legislator knows less and cares less about another person's situation than this person herself does, it does not follow that a legislator does not know or care *enough* to be justified in holding a contrary belief about what is in this person's best interest. Perhaps the odds *are* against a legislator's being right in believing that another adult is wrong about what is best for her. The odds are likewise against anyone's being right that a prosecutor is wrong in charging someone with murder. It does not follow that we are never justified in believing that the prosecutor has made a mistake.

Students sometimes suggest to me that it is not possible to be justified in believing that another person is wrong about what

7 Ibid., p. 9.

is best for her because it is not possible to "get inside another person's head." It is not necessary, however, to get inside anyone else's head to be justified in supporting a paternalistic policy. Consider here what justifies us in supporting a *nonpaternalistic* coercive policy, a highway speed limit, for example. To be justified in supporting this policy, we must be justified in believing that someone's reasons to want the government to require drivers to drive more slowly on the highway outweigh anyone's reasons to want the government to permit them to drive faster. We are justified in believing this if (a) we are justified in believing the factual propositions that provide the reasons for the policy and (b) the judgment that these reasons outweigh the reasons against this policy withstands our critical scrutiny. So, if there is good reason for us to believe that a highway speed limit will reduce the risk of fatality, and the judgment withstands our critical scrutiny that someone's reasons to want the government to reduce this risk to her in this way outweigh anyone's reasons to want it not to do so, we are justified in supporting this policy. But if we can be justified in this way in supporting a *nonpaternalistic* policy, we can be similarly justified in supporting a *paternalistic* one. So suppose we are justified in believing that wearing a helmet significantly reduces a motorcyclist's risk of death or permanent brain damage, and the judgment withstands our critical scrutiny that this reason for a motorcyclist to want a helmet law outweighs his reason not to want it. Then we are likewise justified in supporting this policy, even though it is paternalistic. In short, if it is not necessary to get inside the heads of *two different people* in order to be justified in supporting a nonpaternalistic policy that limits the liberty of one of them for the benefit of the other, it is likewise unnecessary to get inside the head of *one person* in order to be justified in supporting a paternalistic policy that limits a person's liberty for his own benefit. For these reasons I do not think that the epistemic worries that attend the argument for drug prohibition should be understood as special worries about paternalism.

This is not to deny that there are reasonable epistemic concerns about the justification of drug laws. Personally I believe that we are justified in believing the propositions that constitute the strongest case for heroin prohibition, but perhaps I am wrong. If so, I still hope to have made out the following claim: that if we *were* justified in believing these propositions, and the relevant judgments about the relative moral weight of all the relevant reasons *were* to withstand our critical scrutiny, then we would be justified in believing that some forms of drug prohibition are justified. Obviously we need to know more about human psychology and our social world to be *certain* of the relevant empirical assumptions. What I have done here is provide a nonutilitarian moral framework in which a policy of drug prohibition might be fully justified, given these assumptions, by explaining why, if they are true, drug prohibition, at least in certain forms, violates no one's moral rights or any other fundamental principle of liberal political morality. This is certainly not the last step in defending drug prohibition, but it is nonetheless a very important first step.

Further Readings

Booth, Martin. *Opium: A History*. New York: St. Martin's Press, 1998.

Brecher, Edward M., and the Editors of Consumer Reports. *Licit and Illicit Drugs*. Boston: Little, Brown, 1972.

Cohen, Jay S. *Overdose: The Case against the Drug Companies*. New York: Jeremy P. Tarcher/Putnam, 2001.

Courtwright, David T. *Forces of Habit: Drugs and the Making of the Modern World*. Cambridge, MA: Harvard University Press, 2001.

Currie, Elliott. *Reckoning: Drugs, the Cities, and the American Future*. New York: Hill & Wang, 1993.

Davenport-Hines, Richard. *The Pursuit of Oblivion: A Global History of Narcotics 1500–2000*. London: Weidenfeld & Nicolson, 2001.

Earlywine, Mitch. *Understanding Marijuana: A New Look at the Scientific Evidence*. Oxford: Oxford University Press, 2002.

Fish, Jefferson, ed. *How to Legalize Drugs*. Northvale, NJ: Jason Aronson, 1998.

Goode, Erich. *Drugs in American Society*, 5th ed. New York: McGraw-Hill, 1999.

Heymann, Philip B., and Brownsberger, William N., eds. *Drug Addiction and Drug Policy: The Struggle to Control Dependence*. Cambridge, MA: Harvard University Press, 2001.

Husak, Douglas. *Drugs and Rights*. Cambridge: Cambridge University Press, 1992.

Husak, Douglas. *Legalize This!* London: Verso, 2002.

Inciardi, James A., and Karen McElrath, eds. *The American Drug Scene*, 4th ed. Los Angeles: Roxbury, 2004.

Kaplan, John. *The Hardest Drug: Heroin and Public Policy*. Chicago: University of Chicago Press, 1983.

Kleiman, Mark A. *Against Excess: Drug Policy for Results*. New York: Basic Books, 1992.

Latrou, Jason, et al. "Incidence of Adverse Drug Reactions in Hospitalized Patients." 279 *Journal of the American Medical Association*, 1998.

Luper-Foy, Steven, and Curtis Brown, eds. *Drugs, Morality, and the Law*. New York: Garland, 1994.

MacCoun, Robert J., and Peter Reuter. *Drug War Heresies: Learning from Other Vices, Times, and Places*. Cambridge: Cambridge University Press, 2001.

Mitchell, Chester. *The Drug Solution: Regulating Drugs According to Principles of Efficiency, Justice and Democracy*. Ottawa: Carleton University Press, 1990.

Miron, Jeffrey A. *Drug War Crimes: The Consequences of Prohibition*. Oakland, CA: The Independent Institute, 2004.

Musto, David. *The American Disease: Origins of Narcotics Control*, 3d ed. New York: Oxford University Press, 1999.

Parker, Howard, Judith Aldridge, and Fiona Measham. *Illegal Leisure: The Normalization of Adolescent Recreational Drug Use*. London: Routledge, 1998.

Richards, David A. *Sex, Drugs, Death, and the Law: An Essay on Human Rights and Overcriminalization*. Totowa, NJ: Rowman & Littlefield, 1982.

Seal, David Wyatt, et al. "A Qualitative Study of Substance Use and Sexual Behavior among 18- to 29-Year-Old Men While Incarcerated in the United States," 31 *Health Education & Behavior* 775 (2004).

Sourcebook of Criminal Justice Statistics Online. http://www.albany.edu/sourcebook/pdf/

Substance Abuse and Mental Health Services Administration. *The 1998 National Household Survey on Drug Abuse*. Washington, DC: SAMHSA, 1999.

Sullum, Jacob. *Saying Yes: In Defense of Drug Use*. New York: Jeremy P. Tarcher/Putnam, 2003.

Weil, Andrew. *The Natural Mind*, 2d ed. Boston: Houghton Mifflin, 1986.

Zimmer, Lynn, and John Morgan. *Marijuana Myths, Marijuana Facts*. New York: Lindesmith Center, 1997.

Zimring, Franklin E., and Gordon Hawkins. *The Search for Rational Drug Control*. Cambridge: Cambridge University Press, 1992.

Index